HAZEL ARNOLD was born in Dorset but br
where, following university, she taught in schools
another teacher. Though her main subject was I
drama and art was particularly useful and plea
finally taught in a junior school.

As their two children reached late teens and disaffection with the
education system grew, they moved to Dartmoor and opened a small guest
house, catering for walkers and school parties. At that time, life was enlivened
by two ponies, two cats and a rolling cast of chickens, and, of course, walks
on Dartmoor.

Hazel has played in a string quartet, sung in a local choir and belongs
to an art group. She is an avid reader who sews, cooks and, more recently,
much enjoys writing, thanks in part to an invitation to join a writers' group
– the Inkspots.

To Ann
With so much thankes
for all your encouragement
and love
from
Hazel

Under One Sky

A Memoir

Hazel Arnold

SilverWood

Published in 2022 by SilverWood Books

SilverWood Books Ltd
14 Small Street, Bristol, BS1 1DE, United Kingdom
www.silverwoodbooks.co.uk

ISBN 978-1-80042-218-6 (paperback)

British Library Cataloguing in Publication Data
A CIP catalogue record for this book is
available from the British Library

Page design and typesetting by SilverWood Books

Dedication

This book is for many generations of my family and for friends, but especially Ann and in memory of two mothers – Meta and Phyllis.

The creation of this book would have been impossible without the help and encouragement of my family. Firstly, thanks to Henry who for so many years has lived through this project with me and urged me to go to Sweden and Estonia, leaving him with so much to cope with at home. I am greatly indebted to the patient assistance of our son, John, without whom I would never have mastered word processing or the complexities of switching from Amstrad to Word Perfect and finally to Word, with all the glitches that entailed. Many thanks also to our daughter, Ruth, for scanning the photographs, for her cover design suggestions, and for her interest in being yet another generation connected to this story.

Prologue

I came across a folder of letters when my brother and I were clearing out our mother's house after her death. The letters were written in a distinctly un-English hand, with small line drawings at the head of each page depicting buildings in Estonia. I realised at once that they must be from Mum's friend Meta. Mum was not at all a confident person, and it was astonishing that she nonetheless had journeyed across northern Europe to stay with Meta and her family for a memorable two weeks in 1939, reaching home just two weeks before war broke out. I remembered from early childhood how Mum had treasured those letters and that some had made her immensely sad. But I was never allowed to read them. "One day when you are older," she had said, "you shall." So, at last, I read them.

It was these letters that made me want to write about Meta and my mother, and how their affection endured and led to a lasting friendship, and journeys for me too to Estonia and Sweden.

A Croydon childhood

My mother's parents lived in a terraced house backing onto the railway in a part of Croydon called Addiscombe. As a child I found the area very depressing, but it had been Mum's home until she married, so its very familiarity was pleasing to her. The road was immensely long and tedious as we laboured from the bus on short legs past rows of identical houses to number 169. Mum encouraged us by checking our progress against the door numbers, and I absorbed the idea of odd numbers being on our side of the road and evens on the other. Beyond 169 – which was what we always called the house – stretched another quarter-mile or so of road, but I never felt sufficiently bold or inspired to explore. Our grumpiness at the boredom of the walk soon evaporated as Nan swept us in and showered us with love. My brother, Pete, and I were happy if it was a fine day, because we were allowed to climb on top of the air-raid shelter and watch the trains on the lines which ran past the end of the garden. I remember the gritty feeling of the roof on my bare hands and knees and the triumph when passengers waved to us.

Nan and Georgie – as we called Mum's parents – were very different in character but united in their devotion to their daughters, and later to their daughters' families. Georgie was a quiet, intelligent, affectionate man, with a dry sense of humour and twinkling eyes, while Nan bubbled over with warmth and generosity. Their backgrounds were confused and obscure, as neither had been brought up by their own parents. This was probably why they exulted more than most in the increase of the family, as grandchildren were followed by great-grandchildren – all of whom could do no wrong in their eyes. One Christmas when we were all together, Nan suddenly said, as she surveyed the vast family through candles and crackers, "Look, George, this is all our entire fault!" Georgie smiled with equal satisfaction, his eyes narrowing to two delighted crescent moons.

Georgie was an umbrella maker all his working life, and Nan met him when she came to work at the shop, making umbrella covers. Before that, she had spent a happy time working in a baker's shop in Leather Lane in London. She'd had rickets as a child, and as a result was very short; we used to check our growth against her 4'6" height, since it seemed a more realistic target than most of the other adults in the family. I was told that her stature had been a problem in the baker's shop as the counter and the shelves were difficult to reach, although it may have been that her obvious skill with a needle was the reason for her change of occupation. I loved watching her put the finishing touches to an umbrella cover with tiny, deft stitches.

As a boy Georgie grew very slowly, and there was some talk of him becoming a jockey – which he rather fancied – until a late spurt of growth in his teens put a stop to that idea. By that time he'd been in the umbrella trade for long enough to feel settled. His right hand was oddly distorted following an accident, when he'd fallen out of the mulberry tree in the back yard of the shop and had probably broken several fingers but had just ignored the pain as best he could and got on with the job. "It didn't do me any harm," he would say about this and many other events in his sorely deprived childhood.

My grandparents had little money and very few possessions when they got married, but Nan was an excellent improviser. She knew that Georgie loved kippers, and bought some to fry for him as his first meal as a married man. Rather belatedly realising that they didn't have a frying pan, she cast her eyes around for another metal receptacle – and spotted the dustpan. Both it and the accompanying brush were new, so she gave it a wipe and fried the kippers most successfully, much to Georgie's amusement.

In due course their first child was born and was christened Frances Aimée. Georgie used to sing 'Twinkle, Twinkle, Little Star' to her, and somehow the words stuck and she became known as Twinkle or Twink. For some unfathomable reason, when she started school Nan gave her name as Aimée, so throughout her schooldays this was what she was called. In later life she preferred to introduce herself to new people as Frances, but I find it almost impossible to think of her as anything but Twink.

My mother, Phyllis, arrived three and a half years later and was as welcome as Twink had been. She travelled through life with her first name, often shortened to Phyll, and tried to hide the second, Maude, which she hated. Georgie had a pet name for her too – he always called her Pip as a child. I don't remember hearing him say that, but he still wrote to her as Pip until he died.

When Phyllis was only a few weeks old, Nan became very ill – so ill that both the girls had to be looked after by foster parents for some time. Twink stayed with friends nearby and Phyllis was sent to strangers in South Norwood. As Twink was approaching four years old at the time, she could understand a little of what was happening and was able to see her father occasionally. But it was particularly traumatic for Phyllis, since she was separated from her mother, though still being breastfed at the time. In later life she felt that her horror of partings and departures stemmed from this time, and she may have been right.

Nan recovered and Phyll was restored to the family, but she was conscious of a sense of insecurity all through her childhood. Her nightmares always involved losing her parents, and she hated any children's stories in which the parents were mysteriously absent or dead, 'Alice in Wonderland' being a particular horror.

Like many a younger sister, she adored and looked up to Twink. Judging by two oval-framed photographs that hung in Nan and Georgie's bedroom, the two little girls were very pretty – Phyllis particularly so, with her dark eyes and softly waving hair. But Phyllis felt that Twink was all that was beautiful, good and desirable and that her own character left a lot to be desired. From very early on she harboured a quite unjustified feeling of inferiority. As a little girl she was frequently frustrated and enraged by life's injustices. I suspect that the greatest source of her annoyance was being three and a half years younger than her sister. Twink was by nature a placid, happy and unrufflable child who would have been astonished had she been able to read Phyllis's stormy mind.

One childhood crime weighed heavily on Phyllis's mind for many years. She was very jealous of Twink's dolls' pram and often begged to borrow it for her much-loved and rather lumpy rag doll, Ginger. Twink was very good about sharing the pram, but on one occasion dug her heels in and said she wanted it herself. In a fit of rage Phyll snatched the pram before Twink could stop her, sped along the small landing and bumped down the short first flight of stairs. With a flourish, she skidded round the corner by her parents' bedroom and gave one inspired push, letting go of the handle as she did so. Down the stairs bounced the pram, ricocheting from wall to banister rail with the most satisfying clatter and thud, temporarily soothing her angry spirits with noise beyond her wildest belief. Her triumph quickly changed to guilt as Nan rushed from the kitchen in fright, ready to rescue whichever of her darlings lay in a mangled heap at the bottom of the stairs. Phyllis was filled with remorse, not so much for the naughtiness of the act but more specifically because she was sure beyond even a flicker of doubt that Twink would never, never have done such a thing.

Apart from Ginger, the rag doll, there was always a cat to play with, and some, as kittens, were sufficiently long-suffering to be dressed up and wheeled around in Twink's pram. One cat was discovered on the kitchen table, happily playing with little yellow balls of mimosa beside the upset vase. At another time there was a dog too, who expended considerable energy in annoying the cat of the moment. Mostly the cat was well able to take care of herself, but one day she was caught off guard and fled up the stairs down which the pram had bounced, with the dog in hot pursuit. Fortunately for the cat, the bathroom window was slightly open, so out she flew, heedless of the drop – leaving an inch or two of tail in the dog's mouth.

Phyllis enjoyed her primary school, which was only a short walk away, but the girls were not encouraged to linger in the street – home was where they played. Both Nan and Georgie were very firm about this. One lunchtime Phyllis witnessed a horrifying accident. Not far along the road from home was the house and work yard of the local coal merchant, with an arched entry to the yard from the street. The coal merchant, who had been home for lunch, carefully backed his lorry out of the yard, unaware that his small son had run out of the house and was in the way. Phyllis arrived just after the incident and couldn't at first understand what she was seeing. On the cobbled yard lay a pathetically small and indescribable heap which was to haunt her dreams for years to come. She was stunned to realise that a little life could be so abruptly and brutally halted. Nan was appalled by the accident, but she lacked the insight to appreciate just how affected Phyll had been, and consequently didn't give her the sort of reassurance she craved. Georgie was the one who understood Phyll's character better.

Nan had bursts of enthusiasm about various bizarre ideas, from phrenology – the determining of character by reading the shape of the skull – to theosophy, which led to the odd seance at 169, much to Georgie's disgust. She dipped and sipped at various branches of Christianity and was quite happy to move from one obsession to another with hardly a backward glance.

Georgie was very critical of this, and would say "Oh, Ethèle!" in a tone of reproach which particularly annoyed her. Somewhat defiantly she took baby Phyllis to a phrenologist, but didn't broadcast the fruits of the consultation. Many years later the phrenologist's report turned up in a drawer, and Phyllis was quite disconcerted to find how accurate some of the predictions had proved. The comment she remembered particularly was: "an overdeveloped sense of justice." I wouldn't quarrel with that.

Nan was a clever seamstress and happily converted the skills needed to make umbrella covers into creating clothes for the girls. She never required a pattern but simply made things "out of my eye", as she said. They were memorably successful garments – dresses, coats and, later, suits. As adults, Twink and Phyllis would look at the few photos of themselves and exclaim, "Oh, I remember *that* dress – it was a beautiful muted green shantung" or "yellow voile" or whatever. Nan still altered and created garments when she was in her eighties, but by then her taste in fabrics was too flamboyant for her daughters, so they encouraged her to sew only for herself at long last rather than for the family.

Georgie was unpretentious and full of integrity. He was courteous in the shop and as honest as could be. He was a good craftsman too, whose loyalty and hard-working nature were exploited by those who employed him to run the business. He adored his daughters and expected high standards of behaviour from them, but at the same time would have forgiven them anything. When they visited the shop, he might proudly introduce them to a customer if it was appropriate, then before they departed he'd say, "Put your foot up here, darling," and polish already-shining shoes with a discarded piece of umbrella cover, a ritual which continued with us grandchildren.

The working week was a long one, but Nan and Georgie had a social life involving neighbours and friends who became the girls' godparents. There were fairly regular card-playing evenings, which Phyllis hated. She would hear her parents arguing over the bidding in a game of bridge, or crossly analysing their hands, and assume they didn't love each other any more. This made her feel desperately insecure. As a result she had a lifelong aversion to cards and their unhappy associations.

Nan and Georgie were undoubtedly close, but theirs was the sort of relationship that thrived on verbal sparring. They were always poor, but Nan was inclined to bursts of the sort of generosity which led Georgie to dig in his heels and appear penny-pinching. For Phyllis the ensuing arguments

13

were agonising. But there were times of accord and sympathy too. One day Nan was hurrying to finish some sewing and impaled a finger on the sewing machine needle. Phyllis was delighted to see how tenderly Georgie cared for the hurt finger and wiped away Nan's tears. She was so relieved to know that they did love each other – then felt incredibly guilty for feeling pleased, rather than sorry for her poor mother.

Both Nan and Georgie were delighted when Twink gained a place at the grammar school; anything to do with the girls' achievements united them, as they'd had so few educational opportunities themselves. Phyll desperately wanted to follow her sister there four years later. However, when she was ten she developed a serious and painful ear condition and, after days of agonising earache and unsuccessful treatment, it was decided that she needed a mastoid operation, which involved the removal of a piece of diseased bone from behind the ear. Before she went into hospital there was a series of visits to the appropriate clinic, and before one of these visits she committed an act of uncharacteristic naughtiness at school that she kept secret for years. The cloakroom was locked during the day, but she had permission to get the key when it was time for her hospital appointment. She enjoyed the importance of being in charge of the key, and carefully relocked the cloakroom door once she'd found her coat. Just outside the door was a drain. On an impulse she popped the key through the grating and heard it splash as it hit the water. It was a neat and satisfying little crime, and she skipped away across the playground without a care in the world. This was one of the few 'bad' things she did which didn't fill her with guilt, and for some reason she was never connected to the loss of the key.

There followed a long and lonely period in hospital. It was yet another parting from her family that increased her insecurity. Children weren't allowed many visits and were encouraged by the busy nurses to be stoical. There was kindness, but it was perfunctory and fleeting. She longed to have Nan beside her to sympathise with the pain or ease the boredom. Apart from the pain, she always remembered the horrid, muffled crackling sound as the dressing was changed in the wound. She was old enough to understand the feelings of concern that her illness provoked at home in that pre-antibiotics age, and she worried about the anxiety she was causing. Nan and Georgie tried their best to show how much she was in their thoughts by sending letters and, when she was a little better, books. Once Georgie brought a bag of chocolate lime sweets to the door of the ward, but these mysteriously disappeared after she'd eaten only one. She never knew if the nurses ate them, handed them around to other children or simply threw them away, but she fumed over the injustice of it. When she was better still, her family sent her a wonderful wind-up gramophone with just a few little records to play on it. It astonishes me now that such loving parents could have allowed 'Will Ye No Come Back Again' to be one of them. Perhaps it was meant to be taken as a joke. Certainly by the time she told me about it she could laugh, but as a ten-year-old she found it nearly unbearable. The brave face she put on hid, even from Nan and Georgie, just how insecure and lacking in confidence she was.

Just as Phyll reached the end of her hospital stay, there was an outbreak of scarlet fever in the children's wards, and she and the other unaffected patients were whisked off to an isolation hospital at Waddon to wait their turn. Fortunately she didn't catch it, and eventually she was allowed home. However, by this time she'd missed many months of school and, not surprisingly, didn't achieve quite such a high standard in the Common Entrance Exam as Twink had. Once again she felt inferior to her sister and, although her days at the Central School – one step down in the pecking order from the grammar school – were very happy, she never gave her abilities the credit they deserved.

Every lunchtime Phyllis had to go to Georgie's mother's home, and she hated it. Mrs Shaw had a women's corsetry and underwear shop in South Norwood, which she ran with the help of her daughter, Fan, and Fan's husband, Reg. Uncle Reg was a strange man and he embarrassed Phyllis, as he did me very much later on when he was an old man. I remember him always wearing brown corduroy trousers. He used to sit me on his knee and tickle me until I slid to the ground in tears, hoping I'd concealed the fact that he'd made me wet my knickers. Phyllis was, fortunately, too old to suffer this sort of humiliation, but she never felt easy with him. She always wondered how women could bear to be served by him in the shop.

Aunty Fan was an attractive woman but a pale and insignificant character, very much under her mother's thumb. She suffered some sort of nervous collapse in her middle age and spent her last years in a mental hospital, which is why I have no memory of her. Fan and Reg had no children, so Twink and Phyllis were Mrs Shaw's only grandchildren. She was a rather aloof and unyielding grandmother for whom the girls felt only dutiful affection. Phyllis remembered her as a physically and morally corseted lady with very pronounced ideas about behaviour.

The irony of this Victorian strait-laced image became clear years after her death, when Georgie discovered more about his own origins. He was in his late fifties when a copy of his full birth certificate came into his possession and he found out that his mother had never been married. This revelation shocked him profoundly. He had always understood that his father died when he was very small, and this was indeed true. But he had never been told the full story. Strangely, Mrs Shaw, formerly Alice Wildsmith, had confessed some of this to Nan, but Nan had kept it from Georgie as she knew how horrified he would be. Apparently Georgie's mother was in service with a family in the north of England and she and the son of the household fell in love. The family wouldn't allow the young man to marry beneath him, but the liaison continued for several years and they had two children – Fan and, a year or two later, Georgie. Georgie's father developed tuberculosis and was sent on a cruise in an effort to improve his health, and perhaps to sever the relationship; he died on board ship. His family never accepted Alice or the children, but they eventually felt sufficiently responsible towards them to give Alice a small sum of money, which enabled her to set up the shop. She had, in the meantime, changed her name to Mrs Shaw, and had several other live-in jobs where a daughter was acceptable but a son was not. Georgie was placed in a number of children's homes, and then in lodgings, and spent very little time with his mother – or "the old lady", as he called her. He once reduced me to tears by telling me how, one Christmas Eve, all the children in the home were given a stocking to hang up, but he'd been naughty and wasn't allowed to. "It didn't do me any harm," he said. I'm not so sure.

A year or two after Georgie's death Phyllis tried to discover more about his origins, and came close to finding out where Alice Wildsmith had been in service and, therefore, who Georgie's father might have been. The trail led her to a particular village in the north of England, but on the very brink of discovery she somehow lost her nerve and didn't follow up the name she had. She regretted it afterwards, but was never able to resume the search. Unfortunately she didn't leave any written record of her findings, thus preventing me from further research.

If Phyllis had known about her grandmother's past when she was a schoolgirl, she might have enjoyed her lunchtimes more. It would have appealed to her sense of romance to weave stories about an illustrious past and relatives she didn't know. As it was, she couldn't get back to school fast enough, and often begged not to go to her grandmother's – but Nan and Georgie insisted.

At school she had many friends and enthusiastically joined in with lessons and games, though she was no athlete. She earned the affectionate nickname 'Flapper' for a while, as she grew rather tubbier than some of the others. The atmosphere of the school pleased her, and many of the teachers were obviously good. She adored History and English – particularly poetry – and French captivated her, but Maths was a source of fear, confusion and mental blockage. The books she met in English lessons opened up a world of imagination and a breadth of vocabulary that charmed her. One day they were reading aloud around the class, and her eye had run on to a passage containing the word 'picturesque'; she was so sure that this must be pronounced 'picture-skew' that she almost begged to be allowed to read that part. When she heard how it should be pronounced she grew hot with relief that her ignorance hadn't been shown up.

Although most of these childhood years were lived in the town, in the end-of-terrace house backing onto the railway, Phyllis loved to visit the countryside, and there was frequent opportunity for this as her godmother, Auntie Lottie, lived in St John's, near Woking. The girls spent a number of happy summer holidays there, from when Phyllis was about five years old. Auntie Lottie and her husband, Uncle Gerry, had no children of their own and obviously enjoyed borrowing Phyllis and Twink on these occasions. They lived in a house on a common where there was grass, bushes, trees, wild flowers and even goats. Through the common flowed a canal, and on the far side of this canal lived a noisy, poor family whom Phyllis and Twink were taught to consider 'common'. The girls never identified all the members of this intriguing family but used to listen for a raucous scream of "Rosie!" at regular intervals, and giggled and marvelled as they tried to imitate the stridency and accent of that disembodied voice.

It was at Auntie Lottie's that Phyllis began to weave elaborate fantasies about herself, quite unbeknown to the rest of the family. In her imagination she was not the younger daughter of working-class parents but a child of noble birth, reared and ably cared for by kindly artisans. Perhaps this idea was fostered by Nan's oft reiterated cry, "I'm sure I was born to be a duchess!" which enlivened life at 169. I don't know how much Phyll knew of Nan's background and to what extent it influenced her imaginings, but there was certainly ample food for speculation there. Nan's father was, apparently, a Frenchman with wavy auburn hair, as far as she could remember, though her contact with him was brief. As a small girl she was regularly sent to a particular house, where a lady gave her an envelope to take home. When she grew older it gradually dawned on her that this lady was her father's wife and the envelope contained money for her upkeep. She never knew her mother or anything about her except that she wasn't married to her father. Unlike the way Georgie felt about his illegitimacy, this didn't bother her unduly, perhaps because she was fostered from a very early age by two loving, kindly, artistic sisters. Their very name, Shepherd, conjures an aura of gentleness and a scent of the countryside.

Mr Floris, part of the Misses Shepherds' comfortable artistic world, was a regular visitor to 169 when Phyllis and Twink were small. He was a courtly and charming gentleman, not very tall but bearded and white-haired, with a black cloak and sombrero, looking rather like a genial wizard from a children's story. It is from Twink that I've heard about him, but he must have influenced Phyllis in her daydreams.

Phyllis dreamed of her own babyhood spent in palatial surroundings with servants and visitors from exotic foreign parts. Quite how she'd been plucked from these luxurious surroundings would vary according to her mood or the book of the moment, but always her 'real' parents were decently dead; even in her wildest flights of fancy she couldn't bring herself to make substitutes for Nan and Georgie. As she lolled by Auntie Lottie's gate, which led onto the common, a handsome knight would come galloping by, his black cloak streaming out behind him, and sweep her off to happy ever after.

Back at 169 there was no common, or garden gate, but there was a little garden, where Georgie spent his scant spare time growing vegetables and flowers. Despite the restrictions of the tiny plot he was a keen horticulturist, and dahlias, chrysanthemums and roses rioted outside, while in the little lean-to greenhouse geraniums and begonias blossomed, and fallen blooms were gathered by the children and lovingly floated in saucers placed on the windowsills or table. Phyllis always loved flowers, both wild and cultivated, though she never really liked gardening. If she could have waved a magic wand over the borders in the gardens of her adult life she would have been delighted. Latterly, visiting the beautifully planned gardens of stately homes was one of her greatest pleasures; perhaps she revisited there the shining knight and garden gate of her noble childhood.

A country childhood

Phyllis's childhood was always part of me, and very real because she was my mother – and a mother who needed to reinforce her identity with stories of family, which I loved. Meta belonged to me in a different and more creative way. She was part of my imagination.

When I thought of her as a little girl I did not see a real child, like the little Phyllis in the photo on Nan and Georgie's wall, but a fairy tale maiden who flitted through an idyllic landscape and lived in perfect freedom. In some ways this wasn't far from the truth, since her first eight years *were* utterly happy and carefree. She was born in rural Estonia in 1915 and was brought up on her father's farm. Farms, to me, were perfect places, and hers was full of splendidly manicured sheep, pigs, chickens and cows, with not a trace of slurry or mud and never a hint of the butcher's knife. It was always sunny and always harvest time, so the picturesque barns were full of hay and straw, though more sheaves and stooks marched across those charming fields, which were even more entrancingly ploughed into chocolate stripes.

I'd no idea, until relatively recently, about the real Estonia and its struggles to gain and then maintain its independence. But as a child, Meta too was totally unaware of the unrest and enormous changes going on around her. Her world was the farm. Large estates were being confiscated, landowners murdered and deported, peasants brutally put down and farmland redistributed – but it was only later that she knew anything about it. Fortunately, her father's situation remained secure and unthreatened.

Meta's father's farm was large enough to support a number of workers. These servants and their families were a kind of extended family for Meta, and she spent her first few years surrounded by caring adults and their children, who were her playmates. It was a classless little community, with the servants living on equal terms with the family. Meta was the only girl and sometimes quite deliberately used tears to get her own way. But she was usually such a busy, happy child that no one minded indulging her – apart from Erik, her brother, who was three and a half years older and took delight in teasing her. My childhood self sympathised enormously with this, as I too had a brother I could never get the better of; at times I envied my mother her big sister, Twink, as I felt I could handle a virtuous older sister far more easily than an irritating big brother.

It pleased me, though, to hear that Meta had a brother as well as a mother and father, and they were, to me, like wooden nesting Russian dolls: Kustas, Meta's father, was the big one, and inside him fitted a slightly smaller Maria, her mother; next inside and next in size was Erik, who swallowed the little narrower, solid slip of a doll that was Meta. She was indeed a thin little girl, with a pale face and fine dark, wavy hair – just right for my fairy tale.

Both Meta's parents came – so appropriately for my childhood mind – from farming families. They'd acquired land in the nineteenth century, when Estonian peasants were finally freed from serfdom after centuries of being tossed around by various giant powers. Her mother, Maria, was one of a very large family and was sent as a girl to live with an aunt who hadn't any children of her own. This was storybook material indeed. The aunt lived not far from Kullamaa, in the west of the country, and Meta's father, Kustas Tonkman, farmed nearby at Üdrumaa, close to the Teenuse River. How those names thrill me still! They rank with the great, grey-green, greasy Limpopo River of the *Just So* stories and with the Yangtse River, where a duck called Ping spent his ducklinghood in another book.

As in all good fairy tales, Kustas and Maria fell in love. But there has to be a testing time before the happy ending, and it was provided by Kustas's mother, who wasn't at all pleased when Kustas told her he wanted to marry Maria. She thought he could do better for himself by finding a richer wife. But she grew to accept Maria, and Meta was never aware of any tensions between the two women, who were both very warm and loving.

Kustas was an intelligent man and he longed to study and go to university, as Estonian landowners were increasingly able to do. Sadly, his mother felt that they couldn't do without him on the farm, so he had to content himself with that. However, he did manage to study a little on his own, and became increasingly involved with local political problems relating to farming and agricultural interests. Shortly after Estonia was declared independent, his expertise and drive led him to work for the national government in the newly formed parliament. This was tremendously exciting and fulfilling for him, but Maria was not so happy as it meant that Kustas had to live in Tallinn most of the time. He still kept a careful eye on the running of the farm, and visited regularly at first.

Meta was naturally closer to Maria since she was always there ready to encourage and help, but she loved it when Kustas came home. He praised her for helping with the animals, or the harvest, or whatever was going on at the time on the farm, and she was a willing worker, far stronger than she looked. On one of his visits, when Meta was about seven, she could hardly wait for him to hear that she'd actually learned how to milk a cow. But Kustas wasn't at all pleased. In his view, a small girl like Meta couldn't possibly milk effectively and the cow ran the risk of mastitis. Meta felt desperately disappointed and let down by his anger. It was the first time anyone had been cross with her for working hard at something, and she was confused by her father's attitude, when the other adults had praised her. She hadn't really noticed before that grown-up people didn't always agree. This was a disturbing revelation.

But life wasn't usually a serious business. She loved everything about the farm and enjoyed the busy daily routine. There were, as my imagination had predicted, cows, pigs, lambs, horses, cats, dogs and hens to attend to and play with. Meta helped with anything that she could, particularly in the summer, when she was outside almost all the time. Sometimes she played with the servants' children, but what she liked most of all was to spend time with her dolls. For hours on end she dressed and cared for them, imagining her own future family in another farmhouse just like the one she lived in.

In my mind's eye Meta's family were always colourfully dressed, like the Russian peasants in a wonderful book of Russian fairy tales we had; Kustas wore leather boots, loose trousers, an embroidered shirt with wide sleeves and a Cossack hat; Maria had full skirts with bands of embroidery, a laced blouse and red triangular scarf; Erik was a miniature of his father, though the hat was more jaunty and had a feather; and Meta was always in blue, barefooted and sparklingly clean. I know now that Meta would be horrified to be likened in any way at all to anything Russian, since the Soviet Union was for so long Estonia's main oppressor. But I'm enchanted to discover that much of the household sewing was done by a woman who travelled from farm to farm and stayed for a number of days at intervals throughout the year. In summer she made Meta a few cotton frocks, which I still see as blue. In winter the dresses were woollen, comfortable enough themselves but worn with woollen stockings that itched unbearably. I picture her butterfly forays around the farm as a little slower in winter, hampered by those brown, woollen stockings which gathered in alluring wrinkles around her thin ankles. But clothes weren't particularly important to her then. She quite liked the idea of learning to sew, but she was far more interested in what was going on outside than in how she looked herself.

The surrounding countryside was very low-lying, with vistas not of distant hills but of green fields comfortably enclosed by dense forests of birch and pine. I added rugged hillsides capped by briar-enshrined castles; bears and wolves surely lived in those forests, kept comfortably at bay by the manly efforts of Kustas and his workers. Somehow the seaside never featured prominently in my fairy tales, but in the story of Meta anything could be accommodated. Not far from the farm was the sea, with brilliant sandy beaches for summer picnics. Close to the nearby town of Pärnu, Meta noticed how the pine trees leaned away from the sea; the wind had bent them all in one direction like so many ears of corn.

From a very early age, Meta didn't just accept but really delighted in the changes each season brought. Spring meant that the farm teemed with baby animals, and buds fattened and burst. In summer the lilacs rioted and laburnums cascaded with golden colour, replacing the apple blossom of spring. There were flowers to pick and berries later – blackberries, blueberries and cloudberries. Throughout the settled weather of summer all was green and beautiful, then with November came winter, with snow everywhere, everywhere. Meta's delight didn't fade as she grew older. In the winter of 1938, when she was twenty-three, she wrote to my mother, Phyllis:

It is lovely winter weather, rather cold but dry and sunny. I do like Estonian winter. I wish you could see it and love it as well. [...] On Christmas Eve it started to snow and on Christmas Day we had lots and lots of white – pure white Christmas snow.

And in spring the following year:

I am getting quite excited, for I am going to the country to spend my fortnight's holiday at my mother's. My mother is waiting for me and I want to go. There are now such lovely sunny spring days when one can't be in, and wants to be among the waking trees and listen to the first spring birds. Only in the country you can just feel how near is the spring, how near is the birth of new life.

After eight years of skipping happily through the seasons, secure and content, Meta's life was abruptly altered. She was plucked from her tranquil green world and sent to school in Tallinn like her brother, Erik.

It was an unbearable separation at first from everything she loved most: the timber farmhouse and barns of home, the animals, trees, fields and the people – particularly her mother. Maria had tried to prepare Meta a little for her new life by teaching her to read, using an ABC book. Meta enjoyed sitting beside her with a book while Maria got on with her weaving. Also in that final summer a pupil from Meta's new school had come to stay, to teach her how she would be expected to behave at school. This was rather a shock – she was used to so much freedom, and the whole idea of rules and regulations was strange and alarming. That summer the sewing lady had made her school uniform clothes – a lilac frock with a white collar and a black apron. But none of this could prepare her emotionally. How could she really understand just how different her life would be? Some of it seemed exciting, but the strangeness sapped her confidence. Most terrible of all was leaving her mother behind.

As she travelled into the town, the pages of her fairy tale early years shut firmly behind her. It was a straightforward journey, but Meta had never been to Tallinn before. At this point in her life she always merged for me with Heidi, a far more substantial storybook figure than all those fairy tale daughters of woodcutters and farmers. Heidi had feelings and emotions, as did Meta. At first Meta was overwhelmed by the tall and beautiful buildings, the traffic and all the people. It was all so very different from home. Unlike Heidi she didn't have to go and live with strangers, as she simply joined Erik at their father's flat. But it was all very restricted after the farm and, of course, there weren't any animals. She missed the attentions of all the other kind adults who'd been so important in her life until then. There was a housekeeper who did the washing, cooking and cleaning, but she wasn't at all like the women at the farm. And there was no mother. So the smallest nesting doll rattled around uncomfortably inside the largest, father doll.

Fortunately, Meta's days were soon too busy for her to have much time to feel sorry for herself, and she liked to be occupied. It wasn't long before she made friends and began to ask them home to the flat or to visit them in their homes. She hadn't appreciated before how other people lived, and was quite surprised and overawed by the opulent homes of some of her classmates, though the small flats of others felt comfortable and almost familiar.

The school was the first Estonian language school for girls to be established in the country. It was opened on September 9th, 1907, a date still celebrated by some of the former pupils, now spread around the world – in Canada, the USA, Sweden and England. The headmistress, Elfriede Lender, was a formidable lady who was only twenty-four years old when she opened the school. She was a strong, determined woman, ambitious for all the girls who came under her sway and determined that women should play an active role in Estonia. Meta found her intimidating. I see her shrinking behind her desk hoping not to be noticed, her pale face looking solemn and anxious as Mrs Lender towers majestically above, declaiming Latin verbs or geometric theorems. She knew very well that in this environment it wasn't any good turning on the tears to get her own way, or even for a little sympathy. Fortunately, other teachers were warmer and encouraged her interest and enthusiasm for many things, especially English.

Kustas was pleased that Meta was so obviously intelligent, but his encouragement didn't do much to increase her confidence. Uprooted from the farm, she was like a transplanted seedling struggling to re-root in uncongenial surroundings; she continued to grow, but the whole basis of her being was shaken. Her new world was a competitive one, and she felt very anxious when one girl from a farm close to her own couldn't keep up with the pace at school and was sent home to the country. What if the same thing happened to her? Part of her would be so relieved, but how disappointed her father would be – and her mother. In fact, she had no reason to worry about schoolwork, since she managed very well and, unlike some girls, never had to repeat a year. Twenty-six girls started at the same time as Meta, and only eleven finished together ten years later. Meta was one of those.

In the holidays Meta went back to her mother and the farm with great relief and pleasure, but Tallinn gradually enlarged her little world in a way that she increasingly appreciated. Although it was interesting to switch from one way of life to another, the countryside remained the place she preferred.

It was in Tallinn that she first began to understand that Estonia wasn't the safe place she'd always assumed. One dark winter's morning as she walked to school – she was nine at the time – she gradually noticed that there weren't very many people about, which was most unusual. Suddenly she was startled by a series of loud bangs quite close by. Although she'd never heard such a thing before, she was quite sure that it was gunfire. It didn't occur to her to turn round and go home, so she hurried on to school and found it almost empty. Lessons didn't start in the familiar way. No one explained what was happening, but anxious-looking parents arrived to take children home, and someone kindly took Meta home too. At the time Meta was more puzzled than worried, but when she saw her father's ashen face she realised that he'd been very concerned. She later understood that there'd been an attempted coup by the communists, although this meant very little to her then.

(My recent delving into Estonian history places this incident almost certainly on 1st December 1924, when a well-organised communist insurrection occurred in Tallinn. A number of men were killed and many more were injured. The government was motivated largely by Estonian nationalism, but even in those years of independence there was a small scab of communist interest, which the Soviet Union – next-door neighbour and formerly the ruling power in Estonia – picked at and inflamed when possible.)

From that day on, Meta grew more aware that the world beyond home and school had something to do with her; she also began to understand what it was to be Estonian. As a child I wished I were Estonian or Hungarian or Polish – something exotic rather than boringly English. Meta grew proud to be Estonian, even as a child, and later struggled to keep this identity.

But for Meta the problems of Estonia paled into insignificance against the disruptions at home. It wasn't entirely surprising that Kustas and Maria's relationship grew more distant as they continued to live one in the country and the other in Tallinn. Meta, travelling as she did between them, didn't understand these problems at all until she reached adulthood herself. She was aware of and worried about their disagreements, but she was so used to their largely separate lives that she didn't spend much time analysing the situation. All this changed dramatically when Kustas brought another woman, much younger than Maria, to live in the flat. Meta was now fifteen and absolutely devastated. She felt desperately loyal towards her mother and just couldn't forgive her father. At the same time she was fully aware that, as a child, she was powerless to do anything other than accept the situation.

Like the daughters of stepmothers in my fairy tales, Meta disliked her father's mistress, and knew that at the flat she would now have to keep her feelings to herself. Her attitude to her father changed utterly, and she felt he didn't love her any more either. It was also the very worst time in her relationship with Erik; perhaps because he too was deeply upset by Kustas's behaviour and couldn't challenge his father, he lashed out at Meta instead. Meta begged her mother to allow her to go back to the farm as she couldn't bear to be under the same roof as her father and his mistress, but Maria remained severely practical and told Meta that she would just have to stay in the flat because there was no other way. She was anxious for Meta to continue with her education, and this had to be in Tallinn. There wasn't enough money to pay for lodgings somewhere else, and besides – I understand this now – she still loved Kustas.

Maria was apparently so sensible and tolerant, but inside she was shattered and humiliated by Kustas's infidelity. She was in Tallinn one summer's day, shortly after the mistress moved into the flat, when she caught sight of the woman on a bus. All the self-control and good sense she'd shown to Meta deserted her, and she felt suddenly so ill that she had to give up all thought of the business that had brought her into the city and rushed instead to a friend, Meta's godmother. Quite by chance, Meta too called in to see her godmother, and was appalled to find her mother ill in bed with sickness and a migraine. How terrible it was to return to her father's flat and say nothing.

Even before the break-up of the marriage and the subsequent divorce, Kustas hadn't been able to maintain the large farm and a flat in Tallinn, so at some stage Maria moved to a smaller place. Part of the new house was a general store, where country people from the surrounding area could buy clothes and some foodstuffs. It was to this holding that Erik returned when he'd finished school and agricultural studies. I have a photo of the farmhouse and of the hayloft.

For Kustas the second marriage wasn't a great success. He was well occupied in Tallinn but still hankered after country life and bought a mill, with the intention of installing his new wife there. However, she wasn't in the least bit interested in being relegated to the country. She'd spent her childhood there but lacked Meta's delight at being a farmer's daughter, and was none too keen to move away from the bustle of Tallinn. Perhaps Meta's father regretted his decision to end his first marriage. He certainly came to see Meta's mother with some regularity well after the divorce – something not unusual at this end of the century, with divorce so common, but then almost inconceivable.

My childhood self couldn't cope with this part of Meta's life. The books I read had happy endings and characters who were good or bad – and, by the last page, the good ones always lived happily. What had happened to those smoothly rounded wooden dolls? I saw Kustas in two halves now, and one half was painted over in black. "But," I was to hear grown-up Meta say, "I know now that he loved us very much. *I* was intolerant and unsympathetic – you have to forgive young people so much."

Phyllis at work

Phyllis left school at sixteen, with distinctions in History and English and satisfactory levels in all other subjects – except Maths. This meant that she failed to matriculate, as in those days all subjects had to be passed at one sitting. Once again, she felt a sense of failure – softened somewhat by the success in her favourite subjects – and began to cast around for the direction her working life should take. Twink had gone into the Civil Service, and was shortly to be married, but Phyll didn't expect to be capable of passing Civil Service exams, and had ideas of her own anyway. She wanted to be a nurse. The idea of nursing had secretly grown since her experiences in hospital as a child. It had been a terrible time for her, but she'd seen how worthwhile a job it could be. There was something of the crusading spirit too, lurking under her sense of failure, and she thought she'd be able to change the system and shower patients with the sort of sympathy she'd craved as a child.

However, the starting age for nursing then, as now, was eighteen, so there was time to do something else first. With Nan and Georgie's encouragement and financial help, she enrolled to do a secretarial course, and took readily to the demands of shorthand and typing – useful skills which remained with her for most of her life. We used to beg her to take down in shorthand a joke or story we were telling, and then we would marvel at the incomprehensible squiggles and lines she produced on the page – the soft and heavy marks which meant different sounds, and the shapes which could be placed on, under or between lines, depending on the word. It all seemed – and still seems – so very clever to me, and I do hope she was pleased by our very real admiration.

With shorthand and typing under her belt, Phyllis was delighted to find that she could start at once as a special nursing trainee at The Royal Eye Hospital on a course that would prepare her in one particular field. General nursing would come later. She was very excited at the prospect and enjoyed acquiring the uniform, with its regulation starched white aprons and headdress, the plain blue dress, and the black laced shoes so comfortable on her wide feet.

For the first time in her life she had to live away from home, and she found this surprisingly difficult. Apart from a brief and exciting school trip to Paris and the frequent visits to Auntie Lottie and Uncle Gerry, she'd spent very few nights away from the family. It may also be that the hospital atmosphere awoke unhappy and painful memories of her childhood illness – memories she'd suppressed or romanticised.

The work interested her and the patients were fascinating, although she longed to be able to stay and talk to them when making beds, taking temperatures or changing dressings. Much of what she saw was horrifying, for many eye diseases treated there were caused by the squalor and uncleanliness of poor living conditions. A nurse's duties often included delousing and bathing a patient so that medical treatment had a chance of succeeding, at least while the sufferer was in hospital and relatively germ-free. No nurse was ever allowed to stand idle – or to sit down, for that matter. As one task finished another would be listed, even if it was to repeat something that had just been done. Phyll didn't exactly object to the strictness and the heavy discipline, the fearsome matron and starchy sisters, but she constantly felt that there must be something better to do than dust just-dusted windowsills or lockers. She was in advance of her time in feeling that the patients surely deserved more time for reassurance about their eye condition or the family at home or just life in general. There was sorrow, humour and, indeed, fortitude there to which she wasn't allowed to respond, even though she yearned to do so.

The academic side of the course caused Phyll few problems, and she quickly became conversant with the elements of anatomy and the nursing procedures relevant to eye treatment. The human body, either naked or clothed, had never alarmed her, and she was fascinated and pleased to learn the correct names for parts of the body and functions hitherto only mentioned in euphemism. For some of her fellow nurses this was a cause for great embarrassment, but Phyll had always wondered why it was acceptable to name the 'bits that show' but not what was covered by clothing.

As children we would sneak long and stomach-churning looks at the nursing textbooks she kept, or beg yards of bandage so that we could try out the techniques illustrated in another book, and spent wet afternoons swathed in strips of old sheeting like a row of diminutive Egyptian mummies. By the time we were reading the diagnoses, many an illness had become curable thanks to the advent of penicillin and antibiotics, but Phyll's textbooks painted a gloomy picture, which gradually led me to imagine that all illness was terminal. As my nightmares became a regular occurrence, Phyll realised that her children had been dipping into an unsuitable part of her cherished past, and she wisely removed the books and reassured me as only a mother can.

During the weeks of duty in the accident department of the hospital, Phyll observed the different attitudes of mothers bringing in children with damaged eyes. Her heart went out to those children whose mothers raged at their stupidity for having the accident – as though any child would choose to lose an eye by falling on a knitting needle. She noted too how children with sympathetic and encouraging mothers were so much calmer than those whose mothers were hysterical with fear at the child's injuries. One accident was to remain with her for a long time partly because of the simplicity of it: two children were quietly fighting for the possession of the only sharp pencil on their desk at school when one let go, causing the victor to jerk the pencil up straight into his eye, with disastrous results. Once we, her children, were old enough to have pencils she was very strict about their use and more than once told us this cautionary tale, until I felt suspicious of almost any pencil and used to imagine it leaping out of my hand and into my eye, blinding me with one dramatic gesture. Even my children, Phyll's grandchildren, remember how she'd admonish any tomfoolery with sharp instruments with the gentle but infinitely firm comment: "Never, not even in fun." It's become an affectionate, half-joking family phrase to be trotted out on all sorts of occasions – but at least we all grew up aware that eyes are precious and worth protecting.

As the months at The Royal Eye Hospital progressed, it became obvious that Phyll had the makings of a good nurse, and indeed she was the top student of the year. She was willing, and acquired skills on the ward quickly and easily – not just the bed-making, with its careful envelope corners which she found almost aesthetically pleasing, but the washing and general care of patients and the slick but careful changing of dressings. One day the operating theatre was short-staffed, and Phyll was told to go and clear up after the operation. Much of the job was merely a question of common sense, but she was startled to lift a cloth placed over a kidney-shaped dish and find an eye gazing up at her. Suppressing her nausea with some difficulty, she asked what should be done with it, and was relieved to escape to the pathology laboratory and deliver the dish and its gruesome contents to the waiting duty nurse.

Not many nurses looked forward to night duty, and Phyll was no exception. The long nights were a constant battle against sleep, and she worried all the time that a patient might need something beyond her capabilities or knowledge. To spend so much time with very little light and contact with the daytime world didn't suit her temperament at all, and she longed for more normal hours and contact with lively, healthy people.

There was regular but all too infrequent time off. If she had an entire day, she would take the train home with great relief and relax under the devoted eyes of Nan and Georgie. Sometimes Georgie's day off coincided with hers and they went on long, companionable walks together, both in London and in the Surrey countryside near Shere, Gomshall or Whyteleafe. They were very close, and conversation never palled between them as they discussed the news both personal and national, religion, philosophy and Nan's latest enthusiasm. I feel close to them, as Surrey walks were very much my own stamping ground through my teens and for the first twenty years of marriage. In my imagination, as I pushed a pram through suburbia, I could wipe away the housing estates and see the cherry orchards and fields Phyllis and Georgie had known.

Phyll used to go to a local evangelical Sunday School and much of her social life was centred on other church activities. Georgie didn't go to church and Nan, of course, dabbled in various things mystical. It was at about this time that Uncle Gerry's brother, Tommy, who professed an interest in the occult, started to conduct seances at 169. Georgie could indulge in a little grumbling to Phyll, secure in the knowledge that she shared his essential loyalty to the family and wouldn't discuss such things with anyone else. Phyll, for her part, told Georgie about some of the patients and complained about the relentless demands of the ward sister – but she couldn't admit, even to him, just how homesick she was and how depressing and tiring she found nursing life. Gradually, as the year wore on, Phyll became increasingly exhausted and dispirited and conscious of quite severe aches and pains, which she tried to hide. Georgie in particular, and perhaps Nan too, may have seen signs that all was not well, but no one commented, and there was no kind of counselling at the hospital; the attitude there was that illness among the nurses was a figment of the imagination. For some time she'd noticed a stiffness and pain in her ankles, and one morning this was so bad that she couldn't get out of bed to go on duty. She was soon transferred to the nurses' sickbay and became very ill, with a raised temperature and swollen, painful lower limbs. Muscular rheumatism was diagnosed. A consultant many years later suggested that it had actually been rheumatic fever, though she didn't seem to show any sign of the heart problems often triggered by this. Her nursing career came to an abrupt end as the hospital doctor attending her said that she shouldn't even consider continuing with a job which involved so much standing and so great a physical demand.

As she recovered, Phyll was ashamed to recognise in herself a great sense of relief; the shame was caused by a feeling that she'd once again 'failed' in a way that her sister would never have done. Certainly she *had* enjoyed many aspects of nursing, but she knew that she'd been unable to develop that necessary self-protective shell that would have distanced her just a little from the cares of the patients. Her sympathetic nature had made her identify too closely with the suffering and pain, which exhausted her both emotionally and physically, and there was too little time between shifts to follow up interests, relax and remember that other lives continued outside the hospital. Many years later she confided to me that she wondered if the whole illness hadn't been psychosomatic. It's obvious that at seventeen she wasn't ready to leave home and cope with a demanding and strictly regimented job such as nursing, perhaps because her experiences in early childhood were still too fresh – or maybe she was simply too immature. Part of her, though, regretted leaving nursing, and three of her treasured nursing aprons are in my possession still, as is the lovely silver belt buckle and a full-length photograph of her in uniform, looking somehow very vulnerable but impressively neat and attractive.

Looking back, I see that I always thought of her as a nurse when I was little, and she was certainly very good at binding up the hurts of childhood and keeping calm. When I was about three and running barefoot in our small garden, I trod on a nail sticking out of a piece of wood and punctured my foot quite badly – the scar's still there to prove it. Georgie was with us that afternoon and he took me on his knee, holding me very close as my mother, the nurse, cleaned and dressed the wound. I can still hear Georgie's tender voice and feel his bristly cheek rub against mine while Mum worked efficiently and firmly at my painful foot. The terror at what I'd done evaporated quickly, and I remember not so much the pain as the feeling of complete confidence in my mother.

Two years later I was again full of admiration for her when she saved my baby sister from choking to death. We were in an unbearably hot cabin in the bowels of the night boat to Guernsey. The sleeping arrangements segregated men from women, and Pete was old enough to join Dad in the men's cabin. Mum, Rosa, my baby sister, and I were sharing with a talkative lady who seemed to know all about bringing up children. She offered to keep an eye on us while Mum went to the bathroom, and popped two sugar lumps into Rosa's mouth when she started to cry. Within seconds Rosa was coughing and spluttering, and the lady looked horrified. She picked Rosa up, but it was obvious to me that she'd no idea what to do, and I screamed and screamed for Mum. By the time she reappeared, Rosa was blue and the well-meaning lady was in hysterics. Mum snatched Rosa away, upended her and smacked her firmly on the back, then poked her finger into her mouth. I cowered on the bunk and covered my face; it all seemed so terrible that I couldn't bear to watch. Why was she being so vicious to Rosa, who hadn't done anything wrong? And why didn't she say anything? Minutes later, when I could see through my fingers that Rosa was pink and breathing again, I stopped crying to listen to Mum dealing with the lady. I'd never seen my mother so furious, and gradually withdrew my hands to watch properly. It gradually dawned on me that the lady could have killed my baby sister and that Mum's terrifyingly rough treatment was to save her life and not to punish her. How safe it obviously was to be the daughter of a nurse!

I was intrigued – but rather sad – to find in her diary of the visit to Estonia, a good six years after leaving nursing, that she still closely identified herself with nurses. She wrote:

Shared cabin with a nurse from Nottingham who was going to stay with Dutch friends. [...] Spoke usual nurses' gossip about beauty preparations made from ether etc. and of old lady – 'cardiac case' – with whom she shared cabin on previous journey.

Part of her still yearned to be back in the hospital world, where she'd felt so confident of her knowledge and worth, but her 'honourable discharge' rendered her secure against criticism and free to fantasise about what might have been.

Nan and Georgie welcomed her back home with much concern and love. With rest, she recovered fairly quickly in the congenial and sheltered atmosphere of home, though her ankles always had a tendency to swell in hot weather or after standing for a long time. Thanks to the secretarial course and its qualifications, Phyll was able to look for a job locally with some confidence, and she worked first as secretary to a man who ran a small wine shop and then in the office of the Gas Company, close to the Waddon Isolation Hospital site where she'd forlornly waited for scarlet fever to strike seven or eight years before. In this office she gained confidence, blossomed and joined in the banter and teasing which blew back and forth, seasoning the repetitive work. Her immediate boss was an amiable man who obviously took pleasure in his harem of secretaries and delighted in talking about them as he lounged at his desk waiting for a telephone call to be put through. "Mary's wearing blue today – wonder who she's meeting tonight," he would muse. The giggles from the women would have to be stifled in case the caller at the other end of the line was connected and likely to be affronted by sounds of hilarity from a serious place of work. He discovered quite soon that Phyll loathed her middle name, Maude, and was often heard to say distinctly into the phone, "There's old Maudie – pity she drinks!" For Phyll this brotherly teasing and easy atmosphere was a new experience, and she lapped it up, enjoying the camaraderie and joining in wholeheartedly with the jokes and chatter.

Now she had time to be more sociable and had a little money to spend, even after she'd paid her way at home. Her interest in dressmaking was rekindled and, under Nan's guidance at first, then with increasing confidence, she was able to extend her meagre wardrobe and dream up clothing for the future. One day as she walked along the alley which led from the station, full of plans for the money in her pay packet, a man ran past and snatched her handbag. For a moment she was too stunned to do more than watch her bag and money disappear before her eyes, but then she started after the thief, shouting at the top of her voice. Usually there were other passengers from the train following this route home, but for some reason she was on her own until the alley reached the road. Here people looked at her in astonishment then helped her give chase, but the man had gained too good a start and got away easily. Neither he nor Phyll's handbag were ever traced. Some women might have been thoroughly frightened by such an episode, but Phyll's reaction was one of fury that anyone should have had the audacity to rob her like that in broad daylight and so close to a busy street.

At weekends and on some evenings Phyll spent an increasing amount of time at the local Methodist church, to which she'd transferred her allegiance since joining a tennis club there. I love this secular reason for changing churches. Closest of her friends was Muriel, eldest daughter of the minister.

With Muriel, or 'Mu' as she was more often known, she enjoyed a succession of energetic holidays, walking, cycling and youth hostelling or staying in boarding houses in the West Country. A college friend of Mu's called May Tamblyn lived on a farm in Cornwall, and the girls stayed there one year. Phyll returned the next summer on her own, having established a good friendship with May – or were her brothers the attraction? The boys were certainly attracted to Phyll, and one persuaded her to go to the pictures with him on her own. Flattered, she accepted the invitation and embarked on her very first date, carefully dressed and extremely shy of her escort, who was almost unrecognisable in his tidy clothes. In the middle of the film Phyll was horrified by a sudden desperate need to go to the Ladies'. Today it's fairly easy and acceptable to handle such an ordinary call of nature, but then even seasoned ex-nurses were discreet about it. Poor Phyll was doubly embarrassed when she reached the lavatory door and found she had no penny to let herself in. Absolutely mortified – and glad that the darkness hid her blushes – she went back to the auditorium and plucked up the courage to ask the boy for a penny. I've no idea what he thought, but for Phyll the evening was ruined and not to be repeated.

I find it difficult to reconcile this energetic, unattached Phyllis with my mother. She often talked about her active holidays with Mu, but I can't square all this physical exertion with what I know of them both. Mum wasn't physically lazy, and certainly she walked or cycled to the shops for as long as I can remember, but there was never any suggestion that she found exercise a pleasure – at least, not until osteoarthritis put a stop to activity anyway, and then she often wished she *could* walk. Perhaps I'm maligning her and it was the thought of persuading three unwilling children to put one foot in front of the other that put her off. Certainly she was triumphant and pleased to come with my family more than halfway up a mountain in Snowdonia when she was more than sixty years old. She was very mobile then, with two functioning artificial hips. And I do remember a few much earlier family cycling picnics, with Rosa perched on a saddle fixed to Dad's crossbar, Mum and Pete on respectably large bikes and me on my little blue fairy cycle. To arrive at the picnic spot – Banstead Down or Woodmansterne were favourites – was always lovely, but I don't remember enjoying all that uphill pedalling; perhaps I moaned all the way and spoiled it all.

Of course, the Phyllis of the walking holidays was a carefree person I never knew. This was probably the most confident and relaxed time in her life, with no great responsibilities and no gnawing guilt about anything at all. I wish, for her sake, that it could have lasted longer.

After the success of the walking and cycling trips in Dorset, Devon and Cornwall, holidays with Muriel and sometimes other members of her family became a fairly regular arrangement, and Phyll was delighted to find her world expanding to the Channel Islands, original home of Muriel's mother. Phyll had grown up without real aunts, uncles or cousins and was entranced by the wide and welcoming family in Guernsey and the magnificent beaches and peculiar charm of St Peter Port. She was a little overwhelmed at first by the size and beauty of some of the houses in which the relations lived, beside which the romance of Auntie Lottie's house near Woking paled into insignificance. Muriel and her cousins were at home in and on the sea, but Phyll hadn't learned to swim as a child because of her ear problems, and now lacked the courage to learn. She contented herself with paddling in the shallows, delighting in the many attractive shells or the distant view of porpoises cavorting among the fishing boats. Croydon began to seem a little uninspiring after holidays like this, although Nan and Georgie's welcome always made each homecoming worthwhile.

Not only Croydon but the repetitive, undemanding nature of her work had also lost its appeal and Phyll began to think seriously about a change of job. She was very much interested in the church and thoroughly enjoyed teaching at the Sunday School; it was a job that required a lot of planning and reading if was to be done well. However, proper teacher training was beyond both her means and her confidence. Muriel was at this time working at The Methodist Mission House in London and, being fully aware of Phyll's unsettled state, rushed to tell her when a post became vacant. Thanks to Muriel, Phyll soon found herself travelling daily to London and delighting in her fresh commitment at the Mission House and friendship with new and stimulating people. Once again she felt part of something worthwhile and useful, just as she had when nursing. It was here too that she was to make a lifelong, close and poignant friendship that would find her crossing northern Europe just as the continent was poised for war.

London 1938

While Phyll acquired her secretarial skills and nursed, Meta was still at school working conscientiously and showing a real flair for languages, particularly English. Some of her contemporaries planned to continue their studies at university, and Meta was a little disappointed that she couldn't join them. Scholarships could be won to Tartu, Estonia's own university, but a university education was expensive and therefore beyond the means of her parents. For Meta these were already troubled times, with the break-up of her parents' marriage still dominating her emotions, so her disappointment was only slight as she had no well-formed ambitions for herself.

Mrs Lender, the energetic and ambitious headmistress, had followed Meta's progress through the school with some interest and selected her to be part of an educational experiment in teacher training. Until then girls were accepted at the school only from the age of eight, but Mrs Lender planned to establish a nursery department or kindergarten for younger children. The 'nursery' was equivalent to our infant or first school. There was already someone in charge of the younger girls, but Mrs Lender wanted to staff a new class with a teacher produced from her own school. With this in mind, she selected Meta as her first home-grown trainee. Meta was certainly interested in the idea, but she also knew that when Mrs Lender set her heart on something, it was almost impossible to refuse. She had already spent eleven years under Mrs Lender's formidable thumb and was so accustomed to doing what was expected of her that she would have found it very difficult to refuse.

I've often tried to envisage this extraordinary woman, Mrs Lender, and imagine a peculiar mixture of Boadicea and Margaret Thatcher – with their iron determination and powerful, trampling qualities of leadership – and my own headmistress, who was also an innovator but of a much gentler and more humanitarian mould. No doubt none of these come particularly close to the real person, but I don't think I would have liked her, however admirable her ideas for the education and improvement of women in Estonia. It's not difficult to understand how impossible eighteen-year-old Meta would have found it to refuse to do what Mrs Lender wished. Like Phyll she lacked the confidence, but I suspect that Phyll's sense of justice and capacity for indignation and anger might just have enabled her to defy even a Mrs Lender had the occasion arisen.

Fortunately, however, Meta liked little children and was genuinely pleased with the idea of teaching them, even if she wished that the training could be done elsewhere. The course didn't involve going to college; she started straight away in the classroom, observing and assisting, while also attending lectures and being paid a laughably small salary. Her days were full but stimulating and varied, as studies other than the mechanics of teaching occupied quite a large proportion of her time. There's a youthful, energetic breathlessness about this short description of her week: *I am at school from 9am till 2pm. Sometimes I stay longer to make some preparations for the next day. Twice a week I have my piano lessons, twice English, and French almost every day. Twice a week I go to gymnastic lessons. So you see I am quite full up and there is not very much time left.*

Certainly too, the classroom held few fears for Meta. She wrote: *Tomorrow I shall see my children – I am so glad; I feel I need them and I shall have my work.* The possessiveness of *my children* is, to me, highly endearing and reminiscent of the happiest part of my own teaching experience, when I'd become so involved with my own class that it seemed almost like a family extension – though one which, mercifully, didn't follow me home each night.

Meta obviously needed somewhere to live while she trained, and at eighteen she found the prospect of staying on with her father and young stepmother absolutely intolerable, so she accepted her godmother's suggestion of lodging with her. This was a very happy arrangement as long as it lasted, but Mrs Lender once again stepped in with the offer of a free room in her house. It was a very difficult situation for Meta, but she unwillingly accepted.

Phyllis the Nurse

Young Meta

There were a few advantages to living in the Lender household. Mr Lender was a warm and charming man who always championed Meta and was very kind to her from the start. He had none of his wife's hardness, and walked away rather than argued with her. Mrs Lender used to say of him, "It's all very well for Voldemar. He's always so happy and always saying such amusing things – but he hasn't had all the sorrows I have had, and the responsibilities with the children and everything."

When they were first married they'd tried to run a farm but it hadn't been very successful. So Elfriede opened her school, while Voldemar worked in Russia as an engineer on the Murmansk railway. He then lost most of his money and came back to farm in Estonia. In fact, while Meta lived with the family in Tallinn, Voldemar spent quite a lot of his time at their farm in Pirita. Meta had a good relationship with him and grew to view him as a substitute father.

There were four Lender children too: Uno and Henno, the sons, and their sisters, Juta and Ilka. Henno, a doctor, was permanently under his parents' roof, and worked both at Tallinn hospital and with the army. Ilka was very much her mother's favourite, but disappointed her by marrying a farmer. Despite this, Ilka's son, Peep, was the apple of his grandmother's eye. As members of the middle class, Mrs Lender had hoped for educated, moneyed sons and daughters-in-law. The Lenders knew many of the people responsible for shaping independent Estonia; indeed, Konstantin Päts, head of parliament, was Henno's godfather.

The Lender household was not the sort that Meta was used to and she didn't feel very relaxed there, although it was definitely less stressful than living at her father's flat. And in due course there were other things to be grateful for.

Mrs Lender was aware that Meta's experience of the world was extremely narrow, and it was with a view to widening this that she suggested Meta should go to London for a few months to study. Timid, unadventurous Meta leapt at the idea with alacrity but some trepidation, as Mrs Lender negotiated a link with the Froebel Institute, arranging for Meta to attend some lectures each week and visit various schools in London. Mr Lender stepped in and made some financial arrangements for her so that she would have money available there. For Meta it was to be one of the happiest times of her life.

When she arrived in London Meta stayed in a student hostel, where there were many other foreign students as well as English. She found it very strange to be transported into such a different situation with no one to monitor her activities and no fellow Estonians to talk to, but for the first few days she was excited by London and by the lectures she attended, and surprised to discover just how full the training schedule was for teachers of young children in England.

A Swedish girl at the hostel took her under her wing and Meta was glad to have someone to talk to, as she was beginning to feel a little isolated and overwhelmed by the months that stretched ahead, interesting though they promised to be. One morning the Swedish girl said that she was going with some other students to a church service at the Mission House nearby, and explained that the service was usually followed by coffee or tea and that it was a good place to meet other people of their age. Meta was happy to go. Although she wasn't particularly religious, the prospect of the sociable time afterwards appealed to her very much.

The staff at the Mission House used to attend the service too. They made and served the refreshments, then circulated among the visitors. It was a task which at first rather daunted Phyll, as she was shy of the visitors and feared she would have nothing to say to them, but gradually her social confidence grew, and certainly by the time Meta was there she enjoyed it. By chance Meta was one of the first people Phyll spoke to that day, and there, over the teacups, they struck up one of those immediate friendships that are impossible to analyse. Meta responded quickly to Phyll's warmth and interest both in her and in her studies; Phyll recognised in Meta the loneliness that she too had experienced as a student nurse living in a hostel. They arranged to meet the next day, and Phyll went home that evening in a ferment of plans and ideas to which she hoped her parents would agree.

Nan and Georgie listened with their usual interest to Phyll's account of her day, and Nan in particular sympathised with the loneliness of the student her daughter so warmly described. Knowing Nan, I suspect that her sympathy was also seasoned by the fact that Meta came from a country far away; the exotic and the unusual were, for her, distinctly alluring. They can neither of them have been surprised when Phyll suggested that Meta should come and lodge at their house. There had been a succession of lodgers throughout the girls' childhood as the extra money was much needed, so the idea was not so outrageous – except that the house was already rather full. Twink was married by this time and she, her husband and their two little boys were temporarily living at Nan and Georgie's while waiting for a flat to become available. Nan always loved filling the place with people – how well I remember Christmases spent there – although I suspect that Georgie, far more practical, had misgivings about an arrangement which added another adult to an already crowded household. However, Phyll's proposal of giving up her own room and 'camping' downstairs for some weeks just so that Meta could leave the hostel was so much in his own spirit of generosity that there was really little to discuss.

Just a few days later Meta moved to 169, and the months which followed were unbelievably happy. She was made to feel so welcome at Nan and Georgie's and, for the first time in her life, experienced living in a harmonious family. Nan quickly adored her, and Georgie warmed to her and delighted in the friendship between Meta and Phyll. Meta loved Nan and thought of Georgie as a "proper English gentleman – courteous but not too close". He would have been very tickled had he known. She noticed how his face lit up when Phyllis came in, and there was always a kiss. It would have been easy to feel jealous of Phyll and the family closeness, but instead Meta simply became enveloped by it too.

Twink and her husband, Alan, were also very kind, and Meta joined Phyll in doting on the two babies. She loved to see little Michael snuggle on Georgie's lap when he came home from work and sat down to his evening meal. Like a fledgling, Michael would look up at Georgie from the security of the knee and demand "Tea, tea!" whereupon Georgie would administer the ritual mouthful of whatever was on his plate, honour was satisfied and Michael could be persuaded up to bed.

This reminds me of a very similar ritual involving my brother Pete, sister Rosa and me, some years later, on Tuesdays, when Georgie came to us after work. His Tuesday meal was always the same – mashed potato mixed with mounds of grated cheese like milky, curling wood shavings. As soon as she heard his footsteps along the sideway Mum would sprinkle the potato cheese with yet more grated cheese and pop it under the grill, so that by the time Georgie was ready to sit down it was golden and bubbling, filling the house with such a tantalising smell that we children would line up beside him and wait for the invitation to open our mouths. With a delighted chuckle that I can hear now, he selected a generous forkful for each of us in turn, first checking that it wasn't too hot. "There you are, darling," he'd say, and we'd savour our mouthful and feel a glow of warmth which was more than physical.

But we were later grandchildren, as yet undreamt of. The attentions of the entire household at that time were focused on Twink's two little boys. In Meta's letters from Estonia after her stay in England she mentions them often and with great affection: *How are Michael and Tony? My heart is quite aching*, and another time: *They are little deary souls.*

Those happy months were not all spent playing with Phyll's nephews, though, or even attending lectures and observing lessons, engrossing as that was. The social life of Phyll's local church was soon enveloping Meta too and she enjoyed the discussions, tennis and rambles which the young people organised, even if the frequent churchgoing was not quite so much to her taste. According to my father, most of the young men fell in love with her on sight; though she remained friendly and warm, there was also an attractive aloofness in her manner, which slightly puzzled him and others at the time. I remember asking Dad what she was like then and can still hear the almost reverential way in which he said, "Oh, she was a *lovely* girl." His tone conveyed a sort of respect and affection for her which was completely sincere.

Mum told me very few details about this time when she and Meta lived for so long in the same house. Now there are many questions I should like to ask, but it is too late. How often Mum said the same thing about her lack of curiosity about Nan and Georgie's past at a time when they could have told her. But perhaps this is really as it should be, because we all have our own lives to lead, and too much knowledge would cut out the delicious possibility of speculation. So speculate I must about most of their conversations and activities, their confidences exchanged and their hopes and desires. What I am quite sure of is the effect that the friendship had on these two young women; both were essentially timid and lacking in confidence and recognised this similarity in each other. Phyll marvelled at Meta's courage in travelling alone to London and drew strength enough from this to contemplate and then actually travel to Estonia. I'm absolutely certain that, left to herself, she would never have had the courage to journey so far – particularly not on her own. Cornwall and Guernsey were one thing, but France, Germany or Estonia were something else altogether. Meta, for her part, basked in the emotional comfort of this Croydon home and in a freedom she'd never experienced before. It was a new experience to be in a position of strength, and she took pleasure in encouraging Phyll to spread her wings. For the first time since early childhood she could be totally herself.

Meta's return

Suddenly it was all over.

24.12.38
Tallinn, Estonia

Dear Phyllis,
I arrived only yesterday – 30 hours later, and my journey was not a very pleasant one. Still, I am glad to be home and have a rest. Today I shall go to my mother's – just in time to have a nice Xmas Eve. I hope you had a nice Xmas and I wish you all the happiest New Year you ever have had. Letter follows.
Yours Meta

Vaiknal, Estonia

My Dearest Friend,
I am like in a dream. The days are passing and I don't know how I have to live. I wanted and I promised you to write at once, but now I have been already five days in Estonia – and I write my first letter. I hope you received my short notice, that I arrived more than a day and a night later. This journey was an interesting and in the same time a very tiring one. First of all I have to say – I was everywhere late – rather – the trains were late and I had to wait

and wait again and again. The train from Victoria to Dover was late and it was very, very cold in the train. In Dover I went on the boat. We were already late and the boat was an hour longer on the sea. The sea was very rough and the boat was tossing up and down. Almost all people were sea-sick. I am glad I was not – but I had a terrible feeling – a feeling that the world may be wrecked – and I can't do anything and I did not want to do anything. In Ostend the Belgian custom-house officers were very kind and they did not open my cases at all – for I was only in transit. Nowhere but in Estonia, and there only one case.

When we arrived [at the] German frontier we were very late and there was a rumour I have to wait until next morning to get on. But we had great luck and we had an extra train from Aachen to Berlin without any change at Cologne. And I could not have my sleeping-car – even not usual second class. I was still lucky for I had a whole bench. I was with two gentlemen in one compartment – a Pole and a German. They were so very kind that they let me sleep. At Hannover we had to get out and go to another wagon – and it is not clear to me why. And we could not ask because in Germany one can't ask – one has to obey – as the German gentleman told me when I asked. We were in Berlin four hours later and I could not catch the train from Berlin to Riga [capital of Latvia] *and I had to wait twelve hours. I hate Germany – I hate – really.*

It was a good thing that I was not alone – a lady from Riga had to wait too and we spent the time together – at the station because it was so cold – we hardly could go out. We only went a little [way] to have some coffee in a coffee house and then we went into some shops. But the people in Germany are rude and unpolite and I was very disappointed after England.

Still – the time passed and at eleven o'clock at night we left Berlin – again third class and hard wooden seats. But we could sleep – for we had almost a whole compartment for us two. Next day – on Thursday in the afternoon we arrived to Riga and I had to wait some more six hours – alone – in the station. But it was not so bad – and I met some Estonian people.

The third night I had a sleeping-car for I was afraid to be too tired when I get to Tallinn. This train was three hours late and no-one waited for me. I got home safely – only I had no voice. The same day I phoned my mother and told her I am in Estonia. I took a very hot bath and slept twelve hours at a stretch. Next morning I felt much better and in the afternoon I took the train home. At seven o'clock on Christmas Eve I was at my mother's. It was a nice welcome and a jolly Xmas Eve. I lit the candles on my Christmas tree and I was glad to be at home. I felt the same on Christmas Day and Boxing Day and still yesterday – because I had so much to do and to tell and I had here some of my friends who came to visit me. But now when all holidays are over and all people are so busy and I have to be by myself I feel – I wish to be in England. I know I feel this even much more when I have to go to Tallinn to work. There is something in me that seems to have stayed in England – I don't know what this is. But it is the same with everyone who has been abroad and has seen the wide world that he wishes to go back and to live there. One (the person) is divided into two halves.

I am glad – Phyllis – that you are coming in summer-time and not in winter and before Christmas when there are so many travellers. You can take a third-class ticket from London to Tallinn – it is not tiring at all – only – take please a blanket with you on which to lie. Please give many thanks to Mrs Parkinson [Muriel's mother] for the rug was very, very useful. Many thanks to Mrs Shaw [Phyll's mother] for the sandwiches. It was good that I had so many. It was a pity that I forgot all about the flowers that I wanted to give to Mr Shaw. But I was so excited at Victoria.

The Christmas pudding was very nice. I liked it very much and so did my mother. It was a real Christmas dinner.

It is very cold in Estonia. On Christmas Eve it started to snow and on Christmas Day we had lots and lots of white – pure white Christmas snow. It was marvellous to take a walk through the soft snow – I thought of you – I wished you could be with me. But you are coming – you are coming in warm summer, which has its own charm. I love Estonian summer – I wish you could love it as well.

Dear Phyllis – I wish you and your family the happiest and brightest New Year. I thank you all for the good time in England. I feel it was for your sake [thanks to you] that this short time was so nice and enjoyable for me.

With many loves
Yours Meta

P.S. I know my letter is full of mistakes, I hope to write a better one next time. Please give my love to family Parkinson [Muriel's family] and to Miss Gladys and to all the people I met.

This was the first letter of Meta's that I found, and now, on reading it for perhaps the thirtieth time, I still love its energy, intimacy and warmth. But the ironies are inescapable too. *I had a terrible feeling – a feeling that the world may be wrecked – and I can't do anything.* Meta was only writing about the rough Channel crossing, but its further implications are icily apparent in hindsight. Ironic too is the tight-lipped humour of her comments about the delay in Hannover: *we could not ask because in Germany one can't ask – one has to obey.* Not many years later Meta and other Estonians would view the Germans as their liberators. However, what struck me on a much more practical and immediate level was just how badly the description of the journey might have affected Mum, who was intending to follow the same route. After all the detailed description of rough seas, hard benches and hours of waiting, I'm not sure how Meta had the audacity to say: *You can take a third-class ticket from London to Tallinn – it is not tiring at all...*

A reply from England must have followed quickly, since Meta's next letter is dated 7th January:

Tallinn, Estonia

My Dear Phyllis,

Many thanks for your letter. I received that only yesterday, for the people here in the town did not forward it, and I came only yesterday in the town. I had a lovely fortnight with my mother and now the life is again everyday life. I came a little earlier [than] the school begin. I wanted to make some preparations and to think a little over what to do. Today I had a discussion about my visit with my headmistress from the kindergarten (not the lady whom I am staying with). It was not a very pleasant one and I feel at once how different is she and what kind of difficulties I have to face. But still – I have hope and I (have great) wish to do something.

Now it is Sunday. I couldn't finish my letter yesterday – I had something to do. I have really a busy time – I wish I could have more days, more time.

I was very pleased when I received a letter from Mr Shaw. Many thanks for you that you bought a flower for him. It was really impolite of me to ask you at first and to forget it afterwards – but you understand me – I was ever so excited leaving England and starting my journey home. It was a surprise that Mr Shaw wrote to me. The more I feel that you really didn't mind my staying with you and the more I wish to come again. But I had to leave and I have to work in my own country. My mother and my brother send your family their loves and asked me to give you their thanks.

It is a lovely winter weather, rather cold, but dry and sunny. I like Estonian winter – I wish you could see it and love it as well. And besides – we have warm rooms [implying, correctly, that the rooms in England weren't] *and we are warm when we go out. Tomorrow I shall see my children – I am so glad, I feel I need them and I shall have my work. When I write my next letter to you I have to tell you more news.*

Please give my loves to your family and to all whom I know and at Mission House.

I wish you the best,
Yours Meta.

Meta had to wait longer than she wished for a reply, though the letter was apparently worth waiting for:

30.1.39
Tallinn, Estonia, Köhleri 16-3

My dear, dear Phyllis,

Many thanks for your such a long and lovely letter. I was very glad to receive it, for I was really wondering why you didn't write to me. I can understand you very well that you are busy and you don't want to write me a short letter and a long one takes a lot of time. Why is the time passing so quickly? I wish the days could be much longer.

I am not so busy [as] you thought. I am not working any more in the office. I am at school from 9am till 2pm. Sometimes I stay longer to make some preparations for the next day. Twice a week I have my piano lessons, twice English, and French almost every day. Twice a week I go to gymnastic lessons. So you see I am quite full up and there is not very much time left.

Sometimes I am quite unhappy that my colleague does not try to understand me. Sometimes I feel as though she doesn't want to believe me or as [if] she is envying me. Then I am sorry I came over [to England] to see and there is no peace in my heart. It is really difficult – I am afraid to do harm to my children. Perhaps I am not energetic enough to persuade her – but I am alone and she is my headmistress (supervisor) and Mrs Lender (the headmistress of the school) is on her side. I am only afraid that I shall be again the same I was before – and that I don't want. And after some years I can do my best I hope.

I have had quite [a] good time. I have been to little parties and have seen my friends. And my staying in England seems to me such a long, long time ago. I feel myself now much better – I am getting used to the life in Estonia. Oh Phyllis – I am so sorry you can't see our winter. We haven't had a very good one. It has been thawing some days ago, but now we have again a splendid weather and plenty of snow to ski. I prefer to take long walks through the snowy roads. It is marvellous. It is not very cold – rather mild this year. I had to make me a new winter coat. I got a brown one with brown squirrel fur and a warm muff. My brown hat we bought together suits ever so well with my coat.

Phyllis – I am really impertinent or impolite not to send you your money you paid for my books – but I still hope you will come to visit me next summer and I think it is good to find here some money. If you really don't mind – could you send me another book: "Activity Curriculum in the Primary Grades" by Stevens. (I am not quite sure [if] it is Grades or School, but I hope you will find it.)

I haven't had time to read my books. I hope to start in these days, for now I have not to do so many preparations any more and I have seen almost all my friends.

I get quite excited when I think you are coming next summer. I am really waiting for you. I am only afraid – I forget my English and I cannot speak with you so fluently. I have not yet looked for the book I promised to send you – the useful sentences in Estonian and English. I shall try to do this as soon as I can.

I wish to write letters to Mrs Field [Twink] and Miss Parkinson [Muriel], but I haven't yet got time. Please give my loves to them, all the people I know in Mission House and to your family – your dear Mother and Father, who have been so kind to me.

With many loves
Yours Meta.

February passed, with Meta working hard at her teaching and still not seeing eye to eye with her supervisor in the kindergarten. On March 1st she wrote:

My dear Phyllis,

You did write to me – I am so glad – so many, many thanks to you.

Doesn't this picture remind you of your own country – of our ramble together? It is quite near my mother's farm – at any rate it is in the same county – and our counties are small. And you are coming next summer and I can show you many of these places I have on my notepaper – you asked me last time. I wanted so badly to send you this notepaper with a letter to Gladys Dawson but I am too lazy to write. She presented me with a fine picture of the Outwood Mills last Christmas. The time seems to pass too quickly. Sometimes I am quite unhappy that it doesn't stop when we have just our best days to live and to love the life.

A fortnight ago my mother was in the town and we had a good time. I like [it] when my mother comes to visit me. Last week we Estonians had our Day of Independence and we had two days holidays at school. I intended to go to [the] country, but as my mother had just been here I didn't go and I had some rest from my work. But I had some work too – for tomorrow I have to hold a lecture from my staying and life in England. I am lucky – I can do this in my own language. I am so very sorry I have little opportunity to speak English and I think my letters are getting worse, and what will happen when you are coming?

Our winter has been a very bad one in last time. Worse than ever before. All the snow has gone and we have rain and warmth and there can't be any skiing or skating or driving a sledge. We all are so sorry for we love our long cold winter and short spring. Now the spring is so long, the days are so dull and foggy and sometimes the weather is very like your weather – just mild and damp. But we still heat our stoves and have warm rooms, we still wear our thick padded coats and high felt overshoes.

I wonder how Michael and Tony [Twink's little boys] are getting on. My heart is quite aching – I haven't written to Mrs Field and asked. But you know from yourself how difficult it is to write.

I went to the travel office in Tallinn and asked for the help books for the English people, who are coming to Estonia, but they hadn't any. I have to make some more inquiries. I hope you will find some German-English travel book for you in London and I do hope that there will be people to help you – who know some English. You really needn't worry at all.

Only a month to work and then we have Easter holidays. By and by I have done something but I am quite unpleased with my work and sometimes I feel so tired and myself so useless. It is so hard sometimes – isn't it? My headmistress (supervisor) and I – we don't argue so much any more, but I feel the silence even more difficult.

I hope your mother and Daddy are getting on quite well and your friends – family Parkinson as well. Oh – there are lots and lots of people I want to write to and to thank for all these glad memories/ opinions they gave me from England and English people.

I have been twice in theatre. It is so cheap in Estonia that we can afford it much more – but we don't go so very often. I have been to the opera. I enjoyed them both very much. It is a pity that in summer when you are coming the theatres have their summer intervals.

I do hope you will be able to write me as soon as you can.
Yours loving,
My best wishes,
Meta

I hope that your ears are quite all right now and you needn't suffer any more. Give my loves to your family and to my friends.

On the last day of March she wrote:

My dearest Phyllis,
I am so glad that you have not yet forgotten me. It seems to me

such an awful long time ago, when I was staying with you in your comfortable and cheerful home. Every day I feel more and more that my visit to England is in the past and it is a pity that [it] is not in the future as last spring when I was looking forward to make a journey. How much more glad I should be if I could do the same this summer. But there is something to wait for – you are coming. I am just thinking when you are coming. I think the best time would be the second half of July – [so] that you can have the August Bank Holiday as well and I suppose the weather will be the best, and in the end of June there may happen something in my life – who knows. But I shall write about that another time, when all is quite fixed and sure.

I am getting quite excited, for I am going to the country to spend my fortnight's holiday at my mother's. My mother is waiting for me and I want to go. There are now such lovely sunny spring days when one can't be in and wants to be among the waking trees and listen to the first spring birds. Only in the country you can just feel how near is the spring, how near is the birth of new life. I hope I will enjoy my Easter, though I intend to do a great deal of work. It is not so easy to be diligent when you are at home. There is always something else to do, not connected with your own work and intention, and afterwards it seems as [though] you have not done anything.

After Easter there are only six weeks left to work in the schools and then our summer holidays (three months) will begin.

You asked about my frocks. They are already finished long ago. Not that I made them – my dressmaker did it. I have been ironing my blue one. The pink one is for summer. Almost everyone likes my striped frock – do you remember that which I bought ready-made.

I have a great petition. My English teacher Miss Rosenbaum wants to come to England this summer. She wants to brush up her English and therefore she would be delighted if she could stay in a family where is spoken a good and perfect English. Only she wishes that this family could be in London near to all museums and galleries and theatres. Dear Phyllis, could you be so kind and make some enquiries? She does not like to go just to a Boarding House. And she does not prefer a very expensive and luxury one. Can you do this for me please?

I am very troubled about your mother, is she any better now? Has she had her operation already? And how is she getting on with all her housework and all that? I received a letter from her and I am going to write her during my holidays. Please give my loves to her and to your dear Daddy and to all my good friends at church and in Mission House. And what about your little nephews? They [are] little deary souls – my best wishes to them and their parents for Easter. Do you celebrate Easter very greatly? We do it, but not as much as Christmas. We dye the eggs and make a fuss about eating them. And we have special foods. One is called "pasha", made of sour milk and cream, and butter, and sugar, and raisins, and currants and all sorts of things. I like it awfully, though I don't know how to make it correctly.

My best loves and wishes
Yours loving Meta.

April passed, with no reply from Phyllis. It may have been that Nan's illness kept her busier than usual at home – or was she, as Meta suspected, getting cold feet about her visit to Estonia?

11.5.39
Tallinn, Estonia, Köhleri 16-3

My dear Phyllis,

I have been waiting for a letter from you, but there has not been any. I am quite sure that you are very busy and you have really no time for writing. I am only afraid that you have changed your mind and you don't want to come to see my country and my people. It would be terrible – really. I am looking forward to see you in July and I shall be very disappointed and sad if you don't come. But you are coming aren't you, my dear Phyllis, aren't you! I make the plans where to bring you and what to show you. My mother is very pleased that you are coming, and she is really sorry that she doesn't know any English or French. I hope – you will enjoy when you come.

There is no book about that what you have to ask – Estonian-English. But I shall meet you at the station. I am quite sure that you can find such a book in German when you go to Cook's office to (arrange) order your tickets. You can take quite surely third class and you will not be tired at all. Only you must take a blanket or something like this with you, otherwise you will get tired of the hard seats in the continental trains.

I shall write you later on to tell you what you can take with you for me – if you don't mind. And this book: Stevens Activity Curriculum in Public Schools – perhaps you can take this then as well. And some tins with pineapples and Pond's cold cream and others, but I shall send you a list of them when I know that you come and when you come.

I thank you very much for the photos of the Sunday School ramble. I remember many of them and I shall not forget them – they have been so kind to me.

I received a letter from England just yesterday. You have already quite spring days with green leaves and flowers everywhere. Our weather has been very cold since yesterday. We all are waiting for warm rain – then it will be all nice and green very soon. Our nights have been cold – we have had night frosts.

I have to work a fortnight and then my holidays are beginning. This year I am really a happy soul, for I have holidays for three months. Our schools are shut for three months. And I don't do any office work as last year. These two pictures [at the head of the notepaper] are the photos of the famous Russian monastery in the south of Estonia, where I have never been, but to where I intend to go with you. And if you don't come so I can't see it at all this year. You see – you have to come.

Before Whitsuntide I shall go to my mother's and I am looking forward to be with my mother. It is so nice to be at home – you know it, you have always had a nice and lovely home. Oh, how often I wish to be with your family, your dear Mother and Father. They were to me like my own mother and father.

I read a very interesting book. I just finished it some days ago – "Gone with the Wind" by Margaret Mitchell. Have you read it? You ought to read it and then we can discuss it when you come over.

I suppose you are not afraid of the international troubles. There will be no war. Don't you believe that?

Every Monday we have lectures in the Anglo-Estonian Cultural Society. Last Monday there was a lecture about the Tower of London with illustrations. This was in English (as always). I enjoyed it very much and it reminded me of our day there. It was a very lovely time to wander about together.

You can come any time in summer, not only – if it is convenient for you in the second part of June. [She surely means July] *There will happen something – you must guess – will you! Next time I shall explain!*

Perhaps her choice of reading gave some hint about the excitement in the postscript – though the next letter, written at Vaiknal, is tantalisingly slow to come to the point.

11.6.39

My dear, dear Phyllis,

I have been very impatient – haven't I – as I wrote you a very impolite letter that you have not been writing to me. Thank you very much for your letter, and for the news about the family for my English teacher. I do hope that you can send me the address very soon, for she is leaving Estonia in the end of June by a cargo steamer (boat). I wish you could have more time to make the one way of your journey by boat.

Today we have the first real warm summer weather. The weather has since been very cold and windy. And just now I am sitting in my mother's garden under the blooming apple trees – a wonderful place don't you believe. All white and pink and a wonderful scent. I feel so happy, so gay – I wish I could share this happiness with you. And therefore I had to take my pen and paper and I started a letter to you.

I hope your mother is feeling well and enjoying her holiday at the Isle of Wight. I do not know how the weather has been in England. Have you had a lovely June? I could not finish my letter yesterday. I have to do it this morning and to post it before midday. My brother has some friends to visit him and as my mother was not feeling well I had to do some housekeeping.

Do you remember – I asked you in your last letter, if you can guess, what is going to happen? I am afraid you can't guess. I have been a very bad friend – I haven't told you – I am engaged to Mr Henno Lender and I am going to be married on June 20th. I am afraid you are a little bit angry with me. But I don't like to make a fuss about me and my things. It was my greatest secret in England. Once I was ready to tell you this in your dining-room, when you told me about Mr Jack Robinson. [Who he was, I've no idea.] *But – I could not – I was so afraid that if I tell about this earlier then it will not fulfil. My fiancé says you are welcome in the end of July. He knows some English and he is glad that you are my friend and that you are coming to visit me. You don't mind when he is accompanying us in our tour in Estonia? But you haven't seen him. Perhaps you don't like him? He is a doctor and engaged in [the] military hospital. But you will see him all in July.*

Will you excuse me? With many kisses to my best friend Phyllis, Yours Meta.

N.B. I can't finish. I have to write you some more about my thoughts. Does your mother remember what she asked me once? She said – "Your people in Estonia have all the same handwriting?" Why then not when it was all the time the same person who sent me the letters so very often. But I said to your mother, that it only seems to her so. I was very impertinent. But it was to me something so great – I could not tell – not even to my best friend – you. We shall have a very quiet wedding – only our nearest relations and then we shall go away for a fortnight. My fiancé can't have a longer holiday now. He is going to have his month holiday in the end of July and in the beginning of August.

How long time can you stay here? Have you got an extra week? I hope you have! I am waiting for you. And we shall go travelling. And we shall go to Finland – to Helsingfors [Helsinki]. *I have never been there – it will be fun. And my fiancé is knowing Finnish quite well – it is good when he is coming with us if you don't mind.*

I have been quite busy with all the preparations for my wedding day. We have our own flat already, but we are going to live there in autumn. We shall stay in summer at his mother's near Tallinn in Pirita. He is the eldest son of my schoolmistress. But he is not so strict as she is.

Sometimes I am very sorry I can't (couldn't) speak with you. I can't have these discussions with you, we used to have in your house. They made me think very hard and they were so very interesting. Now I am staying before a new scene, before new experiences and who knows what may happen. I hope the best – I love him so much and we understand each other so well. We know each other for four years and we have been living in the same house for as many years. And we know our faults and good sides and although I am a little afraid, I am a little uncertain. But I hope the best and I am very happy.

My dear Phyllis – give my best loves to your family and to your sister's family. Perhaps they will forgive my laziness – I haven't written to them. But I have always been thinking the best of all your people, of all England. Now you understand why I couldn't stay any longer, why I can't come this summer.

My mother and brother and Henno are sending their loves to you and your parents. Henno is in town. I am at my mother's for the last days.

Ten days later, on the morning after the wedding – yes, really – she wrote:

21.6.39
Kiidjärve p.a.g., Estonia

My dear dear Phyllis,

I thank you and your mother and Twinkle, and Gladys for these nice letters and kind wishes. I got these letters just in the morning of my wedding day when my mother brought them from her farm in the country to Pirita (near Tallinn), where is the farm of my mother-in-law. I got married in Pirita at home before the lighted (burning) candles and white blooming [...] (I have forgotten the name of these bushes – so I shall show you these when you come – although they don't bloom then) (I have no dictionary with me!)

But I can't just write you about this very day – I am so very happy. I shall tell you all about that when you come over. We left our wedding party two hours after the wedding and went away to [the] south of Estonia to spend our "honey-moon". And here we are now – we two the most happy persons in the world [...]

It is so hot – so very, very hot and we are in a hostel very near to a river and to a lake where we can swim. It is very pleasant.

After a week we shall leave this place and go to my mother's and then very soon after this my husband must be back at his work and we shall go to live in his mother's farm near the sea. We shall have a very nice summer. I am very glad you are coming and so is my husband. We shall have a good time – don't you believe. But now I am too "busy" to write you any more – you will understand me – don't you! My address will be: Pirita p.a.g. Estonia. (Lender is my name) They will forward all my letters.

I hope you will find the address for my English teacher so I can forward it to her as soon as possible.

My husband sends his loves to you and your family.

Yours loving, Meta

22nd June

P.S. Dear Phyllis I finished my ink in that fountain pen with which you presented me, and as there is no ink in the hostel I have to finish with pencil. I am sorry for that.

Today is as lovely as yesterday if even not lovelier. We are just going to the river to take [a] sunbathe and to swim.

Do you know – our host is an old Baltic baron and his wife is keeping the house and hostel. So are things in Estonia – the change of places.

I hope you will write in your next letter the date of your leaving and arriving day.

Yours Meta.

The visit

It amazes me that the visit went ahead as planned, at a time when Europe was in such turmoil, but it's easy to assume that people knew far more of the machinations of governments than they actually did. There's little sign in Meta's letters of any great sense of danger, and no suggestion that Phyll was alarmed by the possibility of war.

Meta had written confidently in May, *There will be no war. Don't you believe that?* But there were signs of European unrest well before Meta came to England: Germany annexed Austria in March 1938 and was reported to be making preparations against the Czechs in May, prompting a warning to Germany from Britain and France. Chamberlain came back from the Munich conference in September proclaiming "peace with honour" – and then stood by while Germany and Hungary divided Czechoslovakia between them in the first few weeks of March 1939. Hitler threatened Poland next, which drew reaction from Britain and there was shifting and jockeying of alliances between various countries in the following months. As early as May 1939 conscription was introduced in Britain.

Yet plans for Phyll's journey and three-week holiday continued. She set off on July 19th 1939, very excited and rather afraid – but not because of the uncertainties of world politics or any threat of war. Her fears were concentrated on how she would manage with no knowledge of the languages of any of the countries she'd be passing through, along with anxiety about getting on the right train and making her connections. However, her need to see Meta again overrode all these fears.

With the carefully stored letters from Meta I found a few faint pencil-written pages in my mother's handwriting, which turned out to be a diary of the visit. At the time I discovered this, I anticipated a veritable treasure trove of observations, descriptions and introspection, although its very brevity should have warned me that this wasn't so. There are various explanations for the incompleteness of the account, the most obvious being that she was having such an enjoyable and full time that writing about it was too much of a chore. Unlike Meta, the student teacher, she had not had to write anything other than letters for a number of years. There's enough in the diary, though, for me to be very glad that she didn't write it in shorthand. Much of it consists of brief notes and initials, some of which I've added to for clarity.

Wednesday July 19th [1939]

Mummy and Muriel came to Liverpool St. Station to wish me 'bon voyage'. The train dep. promptly at 8.15pm. Comfortable corner seat and travelling companions to Harwich were a Dutch girl and a Dutch man (not together) and a middle-aged German gentleman. Arrived Harwich and spent first 1/- on one English porter who shepherded me through barrier and conducted me safely on board to cabin and into hands of kindly Dutch stewardess who spoke English. Shared cabin with a nurse from Nottingham who was going to stay with Dutch friends. She had made the trip before. Spoke usual nurses' gossip about beauty preparations made from ether etc. and of old lady – 'cardiac case' – with whom she shared cabin on previous journey. Cabin terribly hot, but sea not rough, though I had very little sleep on account of heat.

What a seasoned traveller she sounds!

Thursday July 20th

Awakened in port of Hook and said bon voyage to cabin-mate who was catching earlier train than mine. Had last cup of tea for a long time and left ship at 6.50am and was guided through customs (didn't even open cases) and passport office by porter. What a blessing porters are! – and he could speak a little English. Train a super effort – companions – one good-looking German woman (alone) and one German married couple.

Train sped on stopping at Rotterdam etc. in Holland, then over the border at Bentheim, into Germany. Much examination of tickets, passports and declaration of money. Passed through many towns and by stretches of cultivated land. German married couple got out at Hanover. Spent anxious time as we were nearing Berlin, wondering how on earth I should ask for train to Riga. Near Berlin Zoo Station I asked German lady but she couldn't talk in English so she fetched ticket inspector who in turn brought English boy. Oh joy! He was going to Tallinn too!! So Michael Daniels and Phyllis Shaw introduced themselves on Berlin Zoo Station and sallied forth together. He spoke German fluently and we put our luggage in the left luggage office and went out to explore. Thirsty work so we had drinks at a café and then found the zoo. Decided it would be fun and saw lots of animals. Quite a good zoo and some fun! Then further wanderings, food and more wanderings, ice-cream and then back to the station where we played cards till train arrived. [Knowing how she usually hated card games, this is quite a surprise.] *No sleeping accommodation except 1st Class so curled up as well as possible in swell 2nd Class ordinary comp. M. sat so that I could put my feet up and get some sleep – not much!*

Her anxieties are well suppressed and understated, but how relieved she must have been to meet Michael Daniels. Until I read the diary I'd had no idea of his existence, and wonder what on earth he was doing going to Tallinn – or what happened to him. Michael Daniels, are you out there?

Friday July 21st

Queer lunch on train! Arrived Riga about 5.24pm. Queer place – sort of horse traps, few cars, few decent shops. Changed money and found picture house and went in for 50c [?] *each. Wooden creaky seats – 1st film in Latvian or German? Sloppy! 2nd American with R. Dix and D. Costello – good. More wanderings, drinks, cards in station and train at last. Compt. to selves – shut door (wooden no windows to it) and M. and P. were alone for night! (Kept light on though!) M. slept well and snored better. I slept fairly well. More people got in much later and we arrived Tallinn [...]*

9.10am. Saturday July 22nd

Farewell to Michael. Meta there and took me to breakfast in posh coffee house in Independence Square. To Pirita by bus – gorgeous bath – walk in fields to pick flowers for my room – bunch. Besides family, a M. and Mme. Laby there. Also German lady (she went later in the day). In evening Tallinn with Meta and Henno.

Sunday July 23rd

Slept late. Rain. Pirita and on Pirita Yōgi (river) rowing in aft. with M. and H. Ices and saw monastery ruin. (Dissolved about 1538) Met family on our way home and returned to Pirita Pavilion for coffee and cream cakes. Dinner, talk and bed.

Monday July 24th

Rose early – left house at 8am – to Tallinn with M. and H. Shopping then tour of town. Park, old gates in wall, Houses of Parliament. (Henno got us in by courtesy of his friend the Colonel – escort of soldiers!!!) Up tower and fine view of town. Town Hall and museum and lunch at Golden Lion (Savoy Hotel!). Coffee at café in Independence Squ. fine! Visit to old church (see p.c.), old streets etc. Park at K? [Kadriorg] and President's town Palace (former palace of Catherine, wife of Peter the Great) and passed Peter the Great's house (very small). Saw black swans on lake. Back in town – saw M.D. [Michael Daniels] while we were waiting for the bus to go but he didn't see me! Dinner at home – talk – and walk to sea with Meta – wonderful crimson sunset – mist over fields – crickets – swallows. Bed.

Tuesday July 25th

Rose early, caught 7.30am bus to Tallinn and 8.30 train for Narva (N.E. Eesti) Arr. Narva about 1pm. Narva – "end of Europe" – Russian

*fortress one side of river and German the other – really 2 towns – Herman
and St. John. Russian influence seen in many buildings. A frontier town
and now a 'dead end'. Stayed in Peterburg Hotel (2/6 about a night!)*
[I've no idea whether she thought this was cheap or expensive] *opposite
Russian church. Dumped trunks and hurried down to Narva river –
caught steamer for Narva-Jõesuu. Reached N.J. about 3pm and had
lunch at Casino. Called on Misses Luberg, old school friends of Meta's
and went on sandy beach to Pavilion and had coffee and pastries. Meta
and Henno swam – and we took photos.* [I have one of this day.]

   *Had light supper in coffee house and caught bus back to Narva.
Walked round town from Town Hall to "Dark Garden" where are
many trees and saw iron cross commemorating place where Russians
clambered up fortress wall and into fortress. Walked down to Narva
Maastina (?) where road crosses river and is only route to Russia.
Henno described how Estonians surprised Russians and fought
terrible battle there – the Russians, panicking were killed as they
rushed downhill to cross bridge. Then a snow storm came and lasted
4 or 5 days and street was 'river of blood'.*

   *Bed at Peterburg Hotel. Breakfast in little café then to see big
waterfall – not much water as had been shut off – factories use its force
for electricity. Then by car to Russian frontier (railway not road section)
– no cameras allowed and slight difficulties as I am a foreigner. At lane
end 2 watch towers – one Estonian one Russian. Russian one since burnt
down having been struck by lightning. Saw place where 1st Battle of
Independence war was fought – trenches there still – went in these – 150
oaks now planted as 150 men were in battle. Back to town by car and
lunch at officers' club. By train to Tartu and stayed at Hotel Lumivaa.
Short walk round town and supper at students' restaurant. Bed.*

[Dates in diary now inaccurate. My dates, not hers, from now on!]

[Thursday July 27th]

*Up at 5.30 and to Petseri. Breakfast in Russian Inn – typical Russian
by-play – much dramatisation. To Russian Orthodox monastery – saw
old coins and relics – visit to crypt where monks prepare own graves
using no metal but fingers and sticks. If die before grave finished then*

buried in common grave. Monastery in an old fortress and so on a hill.
Petseri recently partly destroyed by fire.

How delightfully knowledgeable she's become about what she calls *typical Russian by-play*. It brings to my mind a whole host of other assertions which Mum used to make about Estonia. For example, the incidence of stomach cancers and ulcers was very low there, something Henno attributed to the regular consumption of soured milk products such as yoghurt. And on an altogether different level, coffee was always served in restaurants and cafés with an accompanying glass of ice-cold water. It occurs to me that all these little disconnected droplets of information that Mum scattered over the years were, without exception, appreciative. Small wonder that I grew up with the idea that Estonia and the Estonians were perfect.

From Petseri to Jarvaas (?). Lovely country and lunch at little café –
walk across fields to home of friends of Henno. Glorious walk through
pine forest and then to river where spent afternoon. Back to friends
for grand supper and conversation and photo – tophole time – back to
station and to Tartu by 9.40 train – bed.
[Did my mother really use that wonderful dated word 'tophole'?]

Meta and Phyllis

[Friday July 28th]

Tour of Tartu in morning – first to University Library where chief librarian showed us several old treasures and picture of Goethe for which Germany would give much money – enough to build another library. Signed visitors' book dating from 1804. Privileged to see many old books in archives and introduced to English lecturer at University (an Estonian). From there to National Museum in former Russian Palace. Saw many interesting things including ancient Arabian coins – only ones in existence (Eesti used to be an old trade route from Arabia to Baltic) – national dress – ancient weapons and agricultural implements etc. and old cottage – art treasures etc.

Lunch in students' café and by bus to Pärnu via Viljandi, a lakeside town. At Pärnu the Grand Hotel people wanted to put us all in the same room! So we stayed at Hotel Turist. [?] Had glorious evening commencing with ride in carriage and much fun over my discovery that driver is a woman (HE is a woman!!) [Presumably the woman driver wore trousers.] *From Pavilion to Pavilion and walk along moonlit sands. Lovely time. Bed.*

[Saturday 29th July 29th]

To market and then gorgeous lazy morning on sands. Lunch and then to Tallinn and Pirita.

[Sunday July 30th]

Up at 6.30 and to Tallinn by taxi and by train to Haapsalu. Visited Henno's cousin there, walked and returned there for lunch. Spent topping afternoon in Uncle William's yacht – more food and then by train to Risti and car to Meta's mother's. Supper, walk, bed.

[Monday 31st July 31st]

Late rising – to marshes by bicycle and then picked berries – back home
for lunch – lazy afternoon sleeping and resting –

…And that is all there is! Phyllis left Tallinn on 7th August 1939. There was certainly a brief trip to Finland on 3rd August as her passport shows – there's a stamp saying 'Helsinki' – and I know that they were entertained there by a very charming friend of the Lender family, a Mr Väino Vartiainen, who had spent holidays in Pirita. Apparently he was particularly – perhaps even embarrassingly – attentive to Phyllis. Once they were back in Estonia, Phyll was so tired that she slept for almost a whole day – after such a whirlwind tour I'm not at all surprised.

Whenever we could persuade Mum to talk about Estonia, what I remember so clearly is her emotion – and it is this which I miss in the diary. For example, I can almost smell the shiny leather of the gun holster that swung in front of her face in the train when soldiers came around to check tickets and passports. She was shocked to realise that the gun was real. Frightening too was the visit to the Russian frontier. In the diary she merely says *no cameras allowed and slight difficulties as I am a foreigner,* but to me she confessed that the place appalled her and filled her with foreboding, rather like Meta's prophetic feelings on the boat: *I had a terrible feeling – a feeling that the world may be wrecked.* She found herself identifying strongly with the Estonian national pride and felt moved to tears by her visit to the trenches, from where 150 men had fought the first Battle of Independence. All her inclinations were towards pacifism, but she nonetheless championed and applauded the efforts and achievements of the men who fought to establish Estonia as a country in its own right.

Something else which horrified her was the idea of those monks at Petseri who had to dig their own graves with their fingers. She told me about this many years later, when she, Dad and my family were on a walk near Shere in Surrey and visited the church there with its anchoress's cell. Our children were fleetingly horrified by the idea of a woman being walled up at her own request, but the sunshine outside and a bridge over a stream, ripe for a game of Poohsticks, quickly distracted them. Mum was very quiet for some time and I thought she was imagining the anchoress in her cell. But the cell had triggered quite a different memory for her – and she talked to me about the monks at Petseri and how they had haunted her as she imagined their torn nails and the awful uselessness of a life spent in contemplating death in that way.

When I first, and rather laboriously, deciphered the diary, with its faded pencilled writing on thin and crumpled paper, I was hugely disappointed. But increasingly I find in it glimpses of the mother I knew. In the little episode with Michael Daniels, *alone for night* in the far from comfortable train from Riga to Tallinn and watching two ill-assorted films from *wooden creaky seats* in a picture house in Riga, I share her delight and amusement. But I want to know far more. How could she just dismiss Riga as a *queer place* without describing it more fully? Even more frustrating are the frequent references to conversations with Meta, giving no information other than *we talked*. The historical references are more fully expressed, reflecting her interest and, at times, awe, but no doubt she feared she'd forget these if she didn't write them down, whereas the conversations with Meta she could easily recapture from just a few notes.

I know that they talked about Meta's married state, and Mum certainly mentioned some of the young men who featured on the fringes of her life and whom Meta had met. Apparently it was George Parkinson's name that cropped up most frequently – Jack Robinson having disappeared into the mists of history. I find myself hunting for any clues which might pinpoint the day on which a conversation took place that I do know something about and in which I may be said to have a vested interest. I can hear Meta's voice saying: "Phyllis, you're in love with George." Mum hadn't fully acknowledged her feelings until that moment.

And thirteen months after Meta's wedding, on 20th July 1940, my parents, George Parkinson and Phyllis Shaw, were married.

Down to earth

War was declared on 3rd September 1939, just three weeks after Phyll left Estonia. Nan and Georgie spent a worrying time while she was away, trying not to be too concerned for her safety as newspapers and wireless news brought consistently disquieting information to 169. It was the thought of her return journey that bothered them most; it took her through a number of countries, most particularly Germany, where it was increasingly unwise for a British subject to be. But all went well.

Phyll didn't appreciate the potential dangers until later. She was aware that border passport inspections were thorough, and this made her a little uneasy and impatient to be home – much as she hated saying goodbye to Meta. But her mind was filled too with the pleasurable anticipation of seeing George Parkinson again and finding out whether his feelings towards her were as Meta suggested – and oh, she did hope so!

Her head was fermenting with impressions – the beautiful buildings, green countryside, strange language, different food, fascinating historical glimpses and the sandy beaches with their naked, bathing children. We grew up knowing how much she approved of the Estonian custom of letting children under ten enjoy water without the necessity of a bathing costume; it appealed to that practical nursing side of her nature, which never disappeared. In contrast, she was rather shocked by the Estonian habit of eating in public, something that is so commonplace now that it's scarcely remarkable. In far-off Croydon it would never do to eat cakes or even fruit on a bus – what if someone saw you? Even when *I* was at school we could be punished if caught eating ice lollies or sweets in school uniform – something my own children find laughable. It seems that Estonians were then far more socially relaxed and not encumbered by as many conventions as the British.

Only the day after Phyll left Estonia, Meta wrote:

8.8.39

My dear, dear Phyllis,

    I hope you are now home safely. It was a great deal hard to send you away. We had a good time – hadn't we? And we miss you a great deal. We have now lovely summer weather full of sunshine and heat and we have still our holiday – "the naughty boy" and myself. He is enjoying his being free – the same as he was enjoying his travelling. But he needs a little to be at home in peace and in laziness. He has in winter a busy time and he has a hard time before, while [she confuses 'while' with the German word 'weil', meaning 'because'] *we are going to our new home, and I am not a very good and experienced housewife. But I try to learn and be a good wife to him.*

    I send you 7 of these [photographic] *negatives. One – in my home before the house – I shall be sending that as soon as possible.* [Presumably this is not one of the seven.] *I want to have two of that to send one to my mother. These are lovely memories of our days spent together in my small and queer country full of misunderstandings for you and for every civilized person from Western Europe. Isn't that so? But never mind – we all are happy and we love our country very much and we appreciate the freedom and the nearness of nature. I know it was hard – difficult for you to understand us – our rudeness and impoliteness, our everlasting eating and so on (etc.).*

    Henno and myself – we are going to my mother's on Friday morning. Next Saturday my father-in-law, Uno and Juta are coming by car to bring us back to Tallinn – to work.

    I wish you all the best. I beg your pardon – if all wasn't as it should be – I hope you understood our life and our circumstances a little – that we are we only for twenty years. [Estonia gained independence in 1918.]

    My best wishes to your parents. Henno sends his love to you.
    Yours loving Meta

P.S. I hope you will be writing to me very soon – about your journey and the life at home. I hope your father is better now. Meta X

Was George Parkinson very relieved to see her safely back in England? I never asked him. But apparently the courtship progressed smoothly – except that Phyll was mortified, on her first official visit to her future in-laws' house as George's young lady, to spill a cup of tea all over a clean white tablecloth. She was more than a little intimidated by the confidence which so much of the family exuded, and a trifle awestruck by the fact that her future father-in-law was a 'minister of religion', as she was to describe him to Meta. Even her long friendship with Muriel hadn't prepared her for what it would be like to become one of the Parkinson family.

On October 15th, two months after her return from Estonia, Phyll celebrated her twenty-fourth birthday. It startles me to find how old Meta and Phyllis were then – they seem from their letters to be so young! But, of course, twenty-three *is* young. There was a birthday letter from Meta, but it contains sad news along with the greetings:

6.10.39
Pirita, Tallinn, Estonia

My dearest friend Phyllis,

Many thanks for your kind letter. I am so glad to hear something about you and your family in these terrible days, when all is so unsettled and worrying around us. Beside the anxiety of all Estonians our family has had a great loss – my father-in-law, that grey-haired old cheerful man, his blue smiling eyes and his good humour? I think you remember! And now he isn't any more among us. He had an apoplexy of the heart. We knew that all might come one day – but still it was too suddenly.

I am so glad that your father is much better now. When you once have felt the nearness of death, then you guess how dreadful it is. You know that I was almost fatherless and I found in my father-in-law so much understanding and so much friendliness – and I can't find that any more anywhere.

We are still living in the country. It is so cold and so weary around us. But there is always so much to do in the country in the autumn.

You must take in all the crops and put all in order for the winter time. I am longing for my own home, but the days are passing and we can't yet settle down. We hope: in the end of October we shall be there. I hope – you will be coming again to my country and you will see how it looks like. All that terrible war can't last for ever. I am very glad I could see England and you and your family, your home. I am glad you came to see me. And there will be peace and happiness again in that big world. Won't you believe so! And I shall come again to your country. I love your country and your people, and I have my best thoughts connected with my staying in England.

I wish you many nice things for your birthday. I wish you much luck, and harmony and happiness. I wish to be with you on that day, as I was last year. We had a good time – hadn't we? I shall be thinking of you on that very day – as I do it every day. But then with much more best wishes and love. I do it so very early, but the post is very "lazy" now.

Give my love to your family and my best compliments to my friends. And all the best for you, my dear, dear Phyllis.

Yours loving Meta

P.S. My Henno sends love and wishes for your birthday

What has happened to the light-hearted, sparkling Meta of all the previous letters? Suddenly she seems overtaken with melancholy, and not just because of Voldemar Lender's death. Before Phyll's visit, cold weather was no problem because *we heat our stoves and have warm rooms*, but now the cold is *so cold and so weary around us.* There is a desperate poignancy too in her awareness of the world around them: *All that terrible war can't last for ever. [...] And there will be peace and happiness again in that big world. Won't you believe so!* Firmly, almost defiantly, she restates two things which have made her very happy, for whatever happens no-one can take these experiences away: *I am very glad I could see England and you and your family, your home. I am glad you came to see me. [...] And I shall come to your country again. I love your country and your people, and I have my best thoughts connected with my staying in England.*

By now it's obvious that postal services between Estonia and England were far from efficient. At the head of the next letter Mum had scribbled:

"Recd. 28.12.39. Ansd: 10.1.40" – in other words, it took about three weeks to arrive. It is possible that Phyll's reply to the last letter was lost – or was she too absorbed with her own affairs to write? No doubt this letter in December made her very guilty if this were so.

7.12.39
Tallinn, Estonia, Kaupmehe 15-3

My dear, dear Phyllis,

I wonder what you are doing now in these days. I haven't got any word from you since September. It has been a long time – and a very difficult time, and there seems as if [it] isn't going to be easier at all. But we have to live and the life is going on.

I am living in my new flat since the end of October. And I am so very happy in my new home. My mother-in-law and my mother have been here, and my relations and friends – so I have had many parties, and we have had a good time. All have been so very interested to see me in my new home – and I hope, they haven't been disappointed. I do wish that you should come one day to visit me. On those foggy days I miss England a great deal. Our weather is in this time very like your weather and it all reminds me of your country and of that time together with you in your family. After all – I was very happy in England – but I had quite a hard time as well.

The other day I went to the pictures. I saw the film: "Goodbye Mr Chips". Have you seen it? I did like it and so did Henno. And I heard again good English – and I enjoyed that all. I haven't had any practice in English since my English teacher left for Germany in the beginning of October, when all the Baltic Germans left our country. We live in historical days. It was history for us – Estonians.

I have my children – forty of them. And we play and sing and we are gay and happy. On 19th of December, we have our Christmas party at school. And then we are free for a fortnight. And then is very soon a year to the day [since] I left England and started the way back to my own country. It has been an eventful year.

My wishes for Christmas are very big – there should be peace in the world – for ever and ever, that the people might live in happiness.

*And many other such wishes. And for you and your family! Happy
time and many nice things and much luck.*

> *Give – please – my love to all the people I know.*
> *With much love and with best thoughts*
> *Yours affectionately,*
> *Meta.*
> *Henno sends his best greetings.*

An air of depression hangs lightly over this letter despite the cinema visit
to see *Goodbye Mr Chips* – of all the unlikely things to find at a cinema in
Estonia – and the happiness with her children in school. There must have
been a great sense of unease as the Baltic Germans left – they'd dominated
Estonia as landowners for so many centuries. But Meta's thoughts, as ever,
embraced more than her own little country, and I'm still moved by the very
simplicity of her words: *My wishes for Christmas are very big – there should be
peace in the world – for ever and ever, that the people might live in happiness. And
many other such wishes.*

By the time Phyllis heard from Meta again, Estonia was under Russian
occupation.

In February 1940 Phyll and George became engaged, and war hastened
their wedding plans. As more and more young men were called into the
army it became obvious that George's turn was not far off, unless the war
were suddenly to come to an end – and that didn't seem likely. Phyll and
George felt that if they were to be parted, they would rather experience a little
married life first, whatever criticism this might draw from family and friends.
However, from some of George's friends there was a delighted response:

CONGRATULATIONS GEORGE!! wrote Elaine, fiancée of an old
schoolfriend, Aubrey. *Aubs had written to tell me of your engagement and I join
him in wishing you both every happiness and the very best of luck.*

This isn't exactly the best if [sic] *times to think of getting married as the
future is so beastly unsettled but don't get depressed will you. I guess we'll all four
be happily married before long and asking one another to house-warming parties!
Just as soon as Aubs gets out of khaki we'll have a rare good "do" and who knows,
if rationing is over, we may have butter on our bread!*

*Anyway, here's to the future – I hope you and Phyllis will be very, VERY
happy.*

Aubs was another son of a Methodist manse. George had spent holidays with Aubrey's family, and later, while Phyllis was holidaying with Muriel, he made more than one trip with Aubrey and Elaine in a wonderful Bullnose Morris car to Scotland and the Lake District.

Aubrey's mother too was pleased:

We had some sort of inkling that something of the sort might be expected! It is always nice to hear of people doing sensible things like this. [...] I wonder when all this horrible war and its attendant wickednesses will end. I hope you will avoid being dragged into it...

To Aubs, who was already in the army and missing Elaine enormously, George had confided both his love and his intention to register as a conscientious objector when his call-up came. Aubrey was reassuringly approving on both counts:

I really am frightfully bucked old chap and have just written to Elaine to tell her the good news. I'm bucked too to hear that you are sticking to your principles in going to register as a CO [conscientious objector, or 'conchie'] *when the time comes...*

It looks as though George and Phyll's engagement inspired Aubs and Elaine to marry without further delay, as within two weeks of Aubrey's letter of congratulations came an invitation to his own wedding.

7.3.40

Dear George,

Getting married on any of the next 3 Saturdays. Can you be a groomsman? Should be pleased as punch if you can manage it. Do say 'yes'[...] We just decided this separation was impossible, so now for the plunge! I'm completely lost with excitement so please be a groomsman and be a pal!

Cheerio and all the best – Aubs

A letter from Elaine followed a few days later, with a definite date and careful instructions for his duties as usher. The instructions are full of bubbly asides and finish with a final note about the pile of hymn sheets she has ready: *I'm going to let you have this lot and ask you to make sure that everyone is handed one as they arrive. (Sort of programme girl idea! Only don't charge 6d. each absentmindedly, will you?!) [...] And I think that will be all – afterwards you can start to enjoy yourself!*

They sound so carefree and hopeful…

There was no possibility of my parents finding a home of their own, though both of them had a reasonable job and, by then, women were not obliged to give up work on marriage. But there were few houses to let, and in any case the future seemed too uncertain for a house to be a priority. Mum continued to work very happily at the Methodist Mission House, while Dad was a local government officer in Croydon. 88 Chatsworth Road was large and very close to both Dad's office and East Croydon station, where Mum caught the train to London, so when Dad's parents offered them a room after their marriage it seemed a sensible idea to accept. It was neither an ideal nor unusual situation but they were very grateful for it; they expected that Dad's call-up papers would come soon and that this would quickly shape the next stage in their life.

Nan and Georgie thoroughly approved of the marriage and were already very fond of George and the Parkinson family, though a little in awe of their education and social standing. Nan might have entertained almost regal aspirations in her imagination but she had no serious illusions and was proudly working class. Georgie always felt that character, not class, was of prime importance. Nonetheless, he was very proud that his daughter would gain Rev. George Parkinson as her father-in-law, well known both in Croydon and nationally in his capacity as chief fundraiser for the National Children's Home. For their part, the Parkinsons had a great regard for Nan and Georgie, and the two families grew very close.

I know less about my parents' wedding arrangements than Aubs and Elaine's, but hope that it was just as happy an occasion. I do know that, despite wartime restrictions, Phyll made a white figured satin wedding dress which I still have and, indeed, wore myself once, aged about eleven, when acting the part of a princess. It's here beside me now, and I marvel at its small size and complicated style, from the square neck, complete with inset ruched panel, and the elegant narrow sleeves and cunningly shaped bodice, to the long row of tiny self-made buttons down the back from neck to hip. The few photos show me a long, floating veil, embroidered at the edge and kept in place by a headdress of little flowers; I have a tiny sprig of these still in a box, together with one of the cards that accompanied a slice of wedding cake. Mum stored these small treasures so carefully that they're still perfect all these years later.

I see from the photo that it was a sunny day, and both sets of my grandparents smile out at me. Nan has drawn herself up to her full height of well under five feet and is resplendent in a dress and coat she must have made herself, topped off with a very jaunty little hat. Georgie's face is partially hidden as he stands so close behind Phyllis; I just know that he was full of pride for her on this day, but he was sad too, for he'd lost Pip to another George. Grandma is there, but her face is in shadow behind my father's back. Grandpa, who took the service, beams warmly above his dog collar, and I hear his wonderful, deep, round voice, full of Durham vowels. There too is my aunt Twink, looking for all the world like a second bride, with her long, light dress and wide spray of pale roses, contrasting with Mum's, which I know were dark red. Just in front of them all are the two 'little deary souls', adorably solemn and suitably polished from the top of their shiny heads to their little white ankle socks. My parents are smiling, it is true, but there is also an air of wistfulness about them – almost sadness mixed with their joy. Mum, and indeed perhaps Dad too, was already dreading the fact that they must part, as Dad would inevitably be sucked into the mechanics of war in some capacity.

There are other photos of the bride in my possession which were taken some time after the wedding. Dad was always a keen photographer and had rigged up a hopefully glamorous drape of curtain against which to photograph himself in the costume of the latest play he was in – and, of course, to photograph his bride. Mum's face looks very relaxed – even amused in one photo – but she is sitting rather stiffly. Apparently the day Dad decided to attempt the definitive portrait was bitterly cold, and he had great difficulty in persuading Mum to get out of her warm clothes and into her wedding regalia, but she obliged in the end.

Too late for the wedding, but tremendously welcome nonetheless, came another letter from Meta:

22.8.40
Pirita, Estonia

I wish you all the best in your new life. It is the best you could ever do. But you feel it yourself, I am quite sure. It is a pity I couldn't come to England for this day, though I promised that last year. I got to know this only two days ago for I received then your last letter written on 7.6.40 with the invitation card. I was greatly surprised because I did

76

not expect it as soon as that. But I am quite sure that once upon a time I shall come to visit you in your own home. It is then when all over the world is peace and happiness. I have still hope for that. Perhaps it will take only a very long time.

We – Henno and I – spent a fortnight at my mother's. Henno had his holidays. It was a lovely time in the country – in peace and harmony. My mother is very much thinking of you and wondering how you are getting on. We were often speaking of that time last year [when] you were staying with us. We – Henno and I – were sleeping in the same loft [where] you were photographed last year. Do you remember? I like these photos. These are such good memories of "the good old times".

Mr Paalna – our old friend – you wrote about him – is living in his new house, but he is having his meals with us. And all the others are living in my mother-in-law's big house. Little Peep – Ilka's son – is running about, telling his stories about cows and horses and dogs. He is a very lively boy and, I am afraid, spoilt a great deal. He is the only child among so many adults. I try to keep aside – for my ideas to educate a child are a little bit different from these my mother-in-law has. And that is enough. Perhaps I can carry out my ideas with my own children – I do hope that.

Perhaps I shall not work in this year – for this kindergarten where I worked is shut. I have many possibilities to have another place – only the working time is too long there. But all that isn't quite sure.

What is your mother doing? I am afraid she is missing you a great deal. And your father? Are they living alone together?

Henno sends his love to you and wishes you all good things in your new life.

My best compliments to your parents and husband and my friends in England. I hope to see them when I come next time to England.

Yours affectionately,
Meta XXX

Mum's friends at the Mission House were delighted for her, and she and Dad received many presents from them and from other friends and relations. They also acquired a few pieces of furniture to be stored at 169 and at 88, little dreaming how long these things would remain in Croydon.

Dad continued to work just along the road from the house, and tolerated the routine of the office more readily now that he had a wife to come home to. He had left school at sixteen without academic glory, feeling that, as the oldest son, he ought to start contributing to the household. Ministers in the Methodist Church were not at all well paid; certainly the house was provided by the church, but it was a large one and running costs were high. It was lovely to have plenty of space for five children – for Dad was one of five – but they all needed feeding and clothing.

At the time when Dad started school his father was appointed to a series of churches in various parts of the country, which meant that the family moved every couple of years. This was the standard arrangement in the Methodist ministry, although the duration of each stay was later lengthened. All the moves meant that the education of parsons' children was severely disrupted, and boarding schools had been founded for the children of Methodist ministers. At the age of seven, Dad was sent to a boarding school in Redhill, run by his aunts, and from there to Kingswood School, Bath. Although he enjoyed much of boarding school life and told us endless tales about it, I often wonder if his academic achievements would have been greater had he lived at home. Perhaps if he'd shown more talent at passing exams he would have been encouraged to stay on at school longer and gone on to university as both his younger brother and sister did – he certainly had the ability. He had an acutely nervous attitude to exams, which dogged him throughout his career. In some ways he was very confident and could inspire confidence, but the very atmosphere of an exam could make his every brain cell shrivel. It seemed so strange to me that he could, on the other hand, memorise parts in plays with great ease, and he showed nothing but delight in performing on stage.

At one time Dad considered the possibility of following his father into the church, but he gave up this idea, though he was for many years a lay preacher, or 'local preacher' as Methodist terminology has it. He remained a committed Christian all his life but was never one to push his beliefs at others. As small children we were surrounded by our parents' religiosity, and some of it was distinctly enjoyable. The ritual of evening prayers meant that you could be sure of their undivided attention for a time, and no doubt we all played on this.

There were certain festivals and services which I loved, and I basked in the sense of belonging to a community and in the social side of church life. But some of it was very boring, and Pete and I weren't very well behaved in church, so we always sat right at the back until we filed out to the children's service. This was unfailingly embarrassing, as the dear lady who took the service had the most pronounced and giggle-inducing vocal vibrato I have ever heard. The stories she told us were all tediously familiar, and our fellow worshippers didn't seem very interesting either. On the way home Pete and I would imitate the teacher's warbly voice and Mum would always tell us off for being so unkind – she couldn't help the way her voice was, and we should be glad she was prepared to take us out of the grown-up service for a while. Dad seldom joined in with this tirade, and even then I suspected that he shared our amusement but didn't dare undermine Mum's authority by saying so. He did agree with our complaints about the insipid hymns we learned, and gave us more to giggle about by telling stories – largely apocryphal, I suspect – of his brothers and sisters being overheard solemnly singing their own version of some hymns. "Angels ever bright and fair" became "Angels over Brighton pier" and "Pity my simplicity" was transformed into "Pretty mice in plasticine", which was always my favourite. So the game was passed on to Pete and me and, sometimes joined by Dad, we would think of even better alternative lines. Mum didn't really approve of this irreverence.

We were later left to make up our own minds about church attendance, although I don't think they expected either of us to defect as early as Pete did. I've often wondered since whether the loss of his teddy bear hastened Pete's agnosticism. We used to be allowed to take a small toy to church with us, and Pete always took Little Bear. In fact he took Little Bear everywhere, and wrote and illustrated stories about him when he started school. I used to beg for the next instalment, and was so impressed by his cleverness. The walk to church seemed terribly long and bad-tempered. It was only just over a mile but we always had to run most of the way, as Mum and Dad were dreadful about leaving plenty of time to get there. The dinner had to be left ready, beef joint in the oven, vegetables prepared and the Yorkshire pudding batter beaten. One Sunday we were even later than usual, and somewhere along that four-minute mile Little Bear dropped out of Pete's pocket. We searched for him all the way back but never found him. Pete was desolate. If God watched even the meanest sparrow fall, why hadn't he looked after Little Bear?

I don't know how Mum and Dad reacted to Pete's defection but I know that Dad felt coercion would be counterproductive. He had raw memories of family prayers in his own home; one day he rebelled and told his father that he didn't want to participate any more, and was astounded and gratified when Grandpa completely accepted this. My own lapse came much later, and I talked about it at some length with both of them. On some points they agreed with me, and our different views were the basis of many a stimulating discussion over the years.

Dad's own creed changed as he grew older and he always welcomed a theological argument, but at the core of his convictions there remained a firm belief in God and a love of his fellow man. It wasn't surprising that in 1941, when he was finally called up, he registered as a conscientious objector. He simply felt that to kill was wrong. Much later, when I was fifteen or so, I questioned him about this. He said that in retrospect he felt his view was simplistic, and that his attitude would later have been somewhat different, even though he remained essentially a pacifist.

All conscientious objectors had to appear before a tribunal to argue their case, and Dad must have impressed them with his sincerity, for his plea was accepted. He didn't really want to have anything to do with the forces, but expressed a willingness to work as a medical assistant or on the land. These offers were accepted at the tribunal, but he was, after all, drafted into the army, albeit to the Non-Combatant Corps.

His army life began at Ilfracombe, where he found himself in the company of many like-minded men, mostly members of religious groups such as Quakers and more obscure sects, including the Assembly of God. He used to chuckle as he remembered Sunday church parade when they were permitted to attend their own particular services and were dismissed from the parade ground by group name: "Quakers, dismiss! C. of E. dismiss! Romans, Baptists, Congos, Meths, Ass. of God..."

At first Mum was occupied with her job during the day, and she wasn't without young company in the evening and at weekends. Indeed, when Dad left for Ilfracombe, her two nephews, the two 'little deary souls' of Meta's letters, were staying at 88, and she wrote to Dad about them in the second of two letters sent to him on his first day there:

We have had a good deal of fun with the lads today. Tony is quite fascinated at Neville's performance on the violin. He was standing with little hands thrust into brief trouser pockets, feet a little apart, mouth open, gazing up entranced as Neville played and then he asked him to play a dance, but he was still so intrigued that he simply wouldn't dance! Then when he'd had his bath, he asked to go downstairs again and so John and Neville played him a special 'number'. His prayers were profound in the extreme. He said, "Father God, take care of yourself while you are in heaven. You know when it is time for us to come to you. Stop the war, stop the fighting. Thank you for all our food, for sugar and butter and margaween and apples and oranges and cosy bed etc., etc." Michael remembered you and asked God to take care of you while you are in Ilfracombe. Oh! And Tony last night asked God to bless the men who dig for victory!!!

Until I found this letter with a number of others in a leather wallet of Dad's, I'd entirely forgotten that his younger brother, John, was still at home at this stage and that they had a music student staying with them. This student was Neville Marriner – later Sir Neville Marriner, the great violinist and conductor, so no wonder Tony was spellbound. Dad bumped into Neville many years later and was rather taken aback to be addressed as 'Uncle' George, as he and Mum hadn't realised that, in Neville's eyes, they were an old married couple; they certainly didn't feel part of the next generation. At the time Mum was still young and still hoping for her fairy tale. But without Dad it wasn't possible.

Phyll's war

Army days for Dad were not so far removed from boarding school and he later admitted, rather guiltily, that he found little difficulty in settling in to that life. He'd enjoyed the camaraderie at school and found it even more satisfying with the men in his unit. There were always other people on tap to talk to and to share thoughts with and, indeed, they had a lot of fun one way or another between the boredom of routine office work, which was for most of them very similar to what they had been doing in civilian life. As a predominantly Christian group they shared prayers and services, but it doesn't sound as though they were a bunch of serious-minded evangelists.

Quite a number of them were interested in amateur dramatics, and performed *A Midsummer Night's Dream* and *Twelfth Night* in the garden of a big house close to where they were stationed. Some of the wives took the women's parts, but Mum was not among them. Dad kept pictures of "The Dream" in an album which fascinated me in my star-struck youth and still holds some appeal now, not least because several of the faces are recognisable as people I knew as I was growing up. Dad's unit was obviously a place where firm and lasting friendships were formed.

Though Mum was not in these productions, she certainly saw the performance of *Twelfth Night*. I remember them quoting more than once the opening lines of the play. Dad, with a strong Scottish accent, would say: "Will you go hunt, my lord?" and Mum would respond, "The what?" which brought the reply, positively saturated in Scottish vowels: "The hairt." They would then both burst out laughing and talk about times when we children were barely dreamt of.

Mum often told me that they made a very positive decision to have a child despite the war and the uncertainty of the future. Apparently there were several murmurings around the family when news spread of her pregnancy. It seems that it was generally thought that they had 'slipped up', which made her very indignant, and her indignation was second to no one's if aroused.

I don't actually know at what point Mum gave up work and became a sort of 'camp follower', as Dad's unit was moved around. It may be that conditions in Croydon and London were increasingly unpleasant, or – and I think this is much more likely – simply that she couldn't bear the separation. By getting lodgings as close as possible to where he was stationed, Mum had a chance of seeing Dad. His leave was unpredictable and often too short to enable him to travel far. For once their squirrelling has let me down, as there are no letters saved from this time. But there is a lovely photo showing them celebrating their first wedding anniversary in summer 1941. Dad, in army uniform, has his arm round Mum in her pretty floral dress. My brother, Peter, was born some nine months after the anniversary photo was taken – which perhaps explains their air of contentment.

Mum talked frequently about Wilcott Manor near Nesscliffe, where she spent some time and grew to love the area. There were other army wives nearby, but it was the friendships with local people which lent such happy memories to her stay there. Once when I was travelling with my parents by car to north Wales, they suddenly took it into their heads to stop at Nesscliffe and have a nostalgic walk around the village and down the lane to the house where Mum had stayed. As they stood reminiscing about which window belonged to what room, the front door opened and a man emerged and asked if he could help. On hearing their connection with the place he asked us all in for a cup of tea, rather to my teenage embarrassment, and they swapped stories with him and his wife. It transpired that he was the nephew of the old lady with whom Mum had lived – she had died some time ago. The couple suddenly became much more animated as they recalled their aunt talking of a lovely young woman who had lived with her, and who had a baby boy. The old lady had been very fond of the little boy, whom they remembered, from photos she had shown them, as having dark hair. My parents shook their heads, as Peter had auburn hair. I was then horrified to hear the man say, "Oh, but the husband was a conchie though." His distaste was so obvious that I was appalled and tried to blot out what my father's response would be. Part of me was very proud that he had stood up for what he thought was right, and another part of me was secretly rather ashamed that he hadn't been a fighting soldier, although I never thought that he lacked courage. After a brief pause, my father simply responded in a firm and assured way, "Yes, *I* was a conscientious objector." There was a long silence before we took our leave – with dignity, it seemed to me – and my ambivalence suddenly resolved in a tremendous rush of pride for my father.

My parents were a little quiet as we drove on, then one of them commented that of course Peter's hair would have looked dark in a black and white photograph, and how nice it was to know that the old lady had been fond enough of him to keep his photo and show it to her family.

In recalling this small episode, which must have taken place in about 1962, I find a series of other words trickling into my consciousness – just little comments of Mum's from long ago. She once told me how sad she was to see how many of the country wives really let themselves go and didn't seem to take any pride in their appearance after they'd married and produced children. It made her determined not to do the same, and she always dressed carefully and kept her hair washed and neatly done. This caused some women on at least one occasion to comment rather snidely about 'posh conchie wives' when they encountered her in the shop. She also had an unpleasant brush with a doctor when she took Peter, aged three, to have his slight squint inspected. The man sized her up, took in the educated accent, the careful dress and pleasing appearance and demanded to know why she was wasting his time when he had really deserving patients to attend to. The injustice of it made her furious, and she retorted that she was existing on an army wife's pay. He softened a little and inquired what unit Dad was in – but Mum's reply made matters even worse, as the doctor obviously recognised that it was the Non-Combatant Corps. His ensuing treatment of Peter was very rough and caused Peter to be terrified of anyone in a white coat – even a barber – for many years to come.

Looking back, I now find it interesting that Georgie was so uncritical when both his sons-in-law registered as pacifists. As far as I know he offered no criticism at all, though this could easily have been an area of conflict between them, since Georgie nursed an almost lifelong sense of failure at not having been a soldier during the First World War. This wasn't through lack of trying, but rather because he was considered medically unfit to fight – strange when you think that he lived to be nearly ninety.

Mum left Wilcott Manor towards the end of 1942. She'd felt happy and confident there, and grew very fit wheeling Peter along the lanes and, frequently, to the top of Nesscliffe, from where the spectacular views over Shropshire and beyond helped to stifle her anxieties about the progress of the war in Europe and the safety of the rest of the family back in Croydon. She was completely absorbed in Peter and felt that he brought a little bit of Dad permanently into her life, and permanence was something she always craved.

Mum's appreciation of her baby's perfection was obsessive and she nursed a constant sense of guilt at having brought a child into such an imperfect world. Even though he was extremely robust, she worried about his health and was over-anxious about his inoculations, especially the smallpox one, which she insisted should be administered on his leg rather than his arm, where the mark would show for ever and mar his beauty. When I became a mother she told me some of her feelings and concluded that she must have been in an almost constant state of tension and mild depression, which can't have done the baby any good.

For the next year and a half Mum moved from place to place, always as close to Dad's unit as could be managed. Most of these wartime homes were in the country, and she loved this. She walked for miles, becoming familiar with surrounding villages, though not always sure of their names since there were no signposts. She revelled in the wild flowers and pored over books to identify them by name, an enthusiasm she passed on to both my brother and me. While at Nesscliffe she learned to recognise birds, not just from their shape and colour but through listening to their song. I always rather envied this, as I've never progressed beyond a handful of birdcalls. It was all a far cry from Croydon, or even Woking and the childhood holidays with Auntie Lottie and Uncle Gerry.

Sometimes she shared accommodation with a friend and there was a happy time with Dad's cousin Dorothy and her small son. She found the repeated packing up and moving depressing, but Mum still felt that she preferred this to the prospect of weeks and months without a glimpse of Dad. For her, the separation grew more burdensome as the years of the war rolled on. Her awareness of the suffering of other wives whose husbands were killed or injured in combat increased her sense of guilt if she felt depressed, and made her less confident about the pacifist stand Dad and so many other men of her acquaintance were taking. To kill was wrong – of this she was sure – but it was equally 'wrong' to be killed. The whole philosophy no longer seemed so simple.

And where was Meta during these two years? Mum had no idea. She'd written to Meta shortly after her wedding, and again several times later, but there'd been no reply. When the last letter was returned stamped Leningrad she felt certain that something terrible had happened.

I looked again at Meta's last pre-war letter and this time read one particular sentence with greater understanding: *Perhaps I shall not work in this year – for this kindergarten where I worked is shut.* There is no explanation and no further comment, but this was Meta's oblique way of recording her loss of freedom under Russian occupation. The Soviet Union had 'incorporated' Estonia in June 1940, having established army bases there in the previous September. Mum would have known this.

I understand her reticence about political comment, but find it hard to accept what she fails to tell Mum – unless she's hinting at it in *perhaps I shall not work...* When I went back and checked details and dates just now, it suddenly struck me that, at the time of this last pre-war letter, Meta was in fact five months pregnant with her first child. She and Phyll were such close friends yet she neglects to share her astounding news, beyond the comment: *Perhaps I can carry out my ideas with my own children – I do hope that.* How could she keep quiet about such an important event? Perhaps she intended to surprise Mum once the baby had arrived, in much the same way as she had surprised her with news of her engagement to Henno. She said then: *I have been a very bad friend – I haven't told you – I am engaged to Mr Henno Lender [...] I am afraid you are a little bit angry with me. But I don't like to make a fuss about me [...] I was so afraid that if I tell about this earlier then it will not fulfil.* Ah! Perhaps that was it. She couldn't tell Mum until she was sure that all had gone well and the baby was there, fit and healthy.

George and Phyllis, 1941

Easthill

By the time she was pregnant with me, Mum's travels had taken her to Evershot, a village deep in Thomas Hardy country. Twink and Alan lived there for most of the war years as Alan, a conscientious objector like Dad, had been drafted into work on the land. Mum was grateful when they offered her a home, and she loved being with Michael and Tony, the two 'little deary souls'. The house wasn't large enough for all of them, and tempers were frequently strained to the utmost. Peter was interested in everything and sometimes delved into things his uncle would rather he'd left well alone. Furthermore, Mum was fiercely protective towards Peter and resented any advice or criticism about his upbringing. None of this was a recipe for tranquillity.

Dad kept most of her letters from this time, 1944 to 1945, when she was in Evershot. At first I wasn't sure whether to read them, but curiosity got the better of me, and I'm so glad I did. I became totally caught up in her painstaking chronicles of daily life and I found in them an emotional facet of my mother that I had occasionally glimpsed but never fully grasped – her love for Dad and the anguish of their separation. The letters are filled with so much sadness and yearning. As a counterbalance to that is her joy and pride in Pete, and then in me as I take centre stage in January 1944.

My arrival was greeted with delight around the family, and Mum's letters are filled with anecdotes about my progress and Peter's expanding world. We children brought her much pleasure, but there's pain too, as Peter constantly asked when Daddy would be there: *Peter talks about you such a lot each day. I keep assuring him you'll come soon and I hope I'm right.*

When possible, Dad cycled from Bulford Camp to snatch his few hours of leave with us, but even this brief time wasn't at all regular and could be withdrawn without much warning. There was no telephone to inform Mum of a sudden change of plans, so the prospect of leave was fraught with tension and could only be arranged by letter or telegram.

On April 7th1944, Dad's birthday, Mum wrote:

My Beloved Husband,

[…] somehow, I can't go to sleep tonight without writing to you. You have been so close in my thoughts all day and I hope, Darling, you are not feeling too restless and unhappy over this ban on our meeting. Your letter did stagger me rather, but I had a feeling somehow that I shouldn't see you again for some time. It wasn't quite such a blow because I had tried to prepare myself for the time when leave would be cancelled for I guessed that time would come soon. The awful realisation keeps coming over me but I'm trying not to think about it too much. I pray that we may both be kept in quietness and confidence and that it won't be long before we can meet again. It is harder for you in many ways, for as I've said before, I have the children to enjoy. Oh, how thankful I am that we have got children – something of each other and God's love for us. Oh, may it be sooner than we dare hope that you will come back to us for always and that we can make our home together.

I must go to sleep now. How I wish you were beside me here. God bless and keep you Dearest and grant us both patience.

All my love – your own Phyll XXXX

But unexpectedly, on this occasion, he managed to visit:

I hope you got back alright yesterday and didn't feel too exhausted. I expect you feel weary today and trust you'll go to bed early. It was just heavenly to see you my Beloved and I didn't mean to greet you with tears but somehow I just couldn't help it. I love you so very, very much and the uncertainty of when we'd meet again was all so awful that to come downstairs just like that and find you there wrenched open a door in my heart that I'd thought to be so well closed. Oh, but I did love having you and hated seeing you cycle away from me. I suppose one day you will come to me and not have to go away again.

And you – I know how hard it all is for you, Darling, and try so hard to help you as much as I can from this distance.

13.4.44

I had your letter this morning. You poor, poor darling, you did have a bad time and I'm thankful for your sake that you were able to get over here as you did. What a relief to know that you[r] "slough of despond" is far behind you. How glad I was that I was able to give you comfort when you came. Oh, my darling I do love you so much and want to help you all I can, so do always tell me when you are feeling miserable. Don't be afraid that you will worry me, for I want to know always how you are feeling.

It was with something like relief that I read of Dad's depression, as I'd always been led to believe that he coped with their separation all the time. The faint smudge of indignation that I'd nursed for many years on Mum's behalf was erased with one stroke. Life was particularly demanding for her at this time as Peter was ill with tracheobronchitis, Twink had a cough, cold and sciatica – not to mention the discomfort of late pregnancy – and poor Tony had burned his hand quite badly by picking up a smouldering twig from the bonfire. But she didn't burden him with that.

However, not much later it was Mum's turn to need support and reassurance. Her apparent confidence vanished, replaced by the familiar sense of failure, only this time it was worse than any previous failures since it involved her capabilities as a mother:

16.4.44

My Darling,
[...] It's now my turn to feel fed up and miserable and my soul has just been crying out for you this last day or two. Oh, I do need you so much to help with our children as well as to have you with me Darling. Peter's cough and cold are very much better now I'm thankful to say, though Hazel has inevitably developed a nasty cold, poor mite. Peter, however, has been so obstinate and fretty and I've

got a wretched cold and just can't muster a lot of patience and I seem to do nothing but rub him up the wrong way and make things worse. He flies into rages so quickly and over such little things and goes down on the floor and kicks and screams. I really don't know what to do with him and the situation is aggravated because he makes me feel so much more desperate knowing how trying it is for Alan and Twink. More than once I've lost my temper and slapped him and it only makes things worse of course. I feel quite unhappy because of the mistakes I've made in bringing up Peter since Hazel came and feel I've served to make things worse for him by my own rages sometimes. Oh, why on earth can't this damnable war end so that we can settle down in our own home together and sort out these problems together. I feel such an utter failure tonight. But don't let me make you miserable because I am. I expect it will all work out, but for me, and I think for Peter, the position is much worse because we're in someone else's house.

Oh, I do love you so much Darling and just ache for you to be here. Yes, it is true that nothing can separate us from each other's love and that the love of God binds us surely and closely together. I think it is partly this wretched cold that is making me feel a bit off colour and clouding my brain. These physical discomforts mustn't be allowed to dim my vision.

God bless you and keep you Dearest and bring you safely to me soon. I hope and expect I'll be in a happier frame of mind next time I write.

All my love, your own Phyll

Dad fortunately managed to engineer another brief visit:

24.4.44

It was heavenly to have you here and I hated to see you go. I missed seeing you somehow when you cycled along Park Lane. I don't know how it was for I went straight to the fence to see you go along. Did you see me? You would wonder why I didn't wave. Peter was standing on the stile to see you. Life is a bewildering thing just now and I feel rather lost now that I've had to see you go again. It is so precious to have you here. I didn't mention your letter while you were here but it was a lovely one to have. I often go over the events of our life together in my mind and find new joy in them. It seems so strange that in the midst of war we have had so many joys together [...] We shall perhaps have even greater [...]

I'm sorry if I always seem to have so many small things to grumble about when you come. I'm happy here and glad to help Twink and shall miss this lovely countryside when the time comes for me to have to leave it. I'm afraid I have to keep my thoughts and feelings to myself so much that when you come they tend to overflow.

I hope you have a good journey back. God bless and keep you Beloved. I love you, love you, love you and do try to look after your children in the best possible way. It's rather difficult being a father and mother.

During this leave they faced and discussed the ever-growing problem of sharing Twink and Alan's house. Their gratitude was becoming jaded because of the lack of space. As all the children grew, the house became more cramped almost daily, and it would be even worse once Twink's new baby arrived. Dad thought that the time had come to look for a place of their own – not that he had any idea when he'd be able to share it with his family. He knew that his former job in Croydon would be waiting for him once the war ended, and news from Europe suggested that it might not now be so long. It seemed most practical to aim for a property back in the south-east, closer to the rest of the family and to the job in Croydon. To this end they placed hopeful adverts in the *Methodist Recorder* and Nan put their names on a housing list, along with the hundreds of other couples desperately wanting homes.

This practical action made Mum's spirits soar:

26.4.44

I've had such an adventurous day. I have been to Dorchester with the two children all on my own! It is a month since I last went to the clinic and I wanted to go again so managed it today. I feared it would be rather an ordeal, but in fact it turned out to be a most enjoyable time. I got all or most of my shopping done this morning and then we had lunch at Judge Jefferies and went straight to the Clinic. I was only about the 3rd one there and only the 2nd one to see the Dr and I then fed Hazel and was out before 3pm so didn't do at all badly. It has been such lovely weather today and I took milk and a few sandwiches with me and we sat in that little park and had them at about 3.45pm so then had plenty of time to go to the station for the train. Hazel didn't mind the day's outing so much as last time and Peter thoroughly enjoyed it all and has been so good. They are both sound asleep now. Peter loved the trains and all the time we were shopping etc. kept asking me when we were going to see the trains again, bless him! While we were waiting at Dorchester station for the train to come for Evershot, there was an obliging goods train shunting and it thrilled Peter considerably and the darling wanted to know if it was the big train Daddy went on! He never forgets you dearest. [...]

I've bought some materials to make Peter's summer suits and some to make a matinée coat for Hazel. I'm very pleased with my purchases. I do wish you were here to see them and that you could have shared my very enjoyable day. How much more enjoyable it would have been had you been with me.

It was grand to hear from you this morning and to know that you reached camp alright on Saturday. It was heavenly to have you. I do love you so much dearest one. Take care of yourself. [...].

P.S. Have just re-read your letter. [...] Yes, I saw the new moon, darling.

You sound so different, Mum. You must have cheered Dad up no end. I'm sorry the pleasure didn't last longer. Dad's precious bike was stolen and this made your blood boil. The gaiety of the trip into Dorchester was eclipsed with one blow:

28.4.44

Why on earth it had to be yours. [...] Poor you, it means you just have to stick around camp I suppose, as I imagine you can't get far without a bike. What a disappointment too for it stops your visits over here completely. Oh, what a hellish business life is sometimes.

Even the hoped-for home of their own seemed less possible, though no less attractive:

My feelings about leaving here are very mixed, but I shall be more than thankful to be on my own in one way. I'm absolutely weary of being told how to bring up our son. Oh darling, sometimes I want to creep away alone and have a weep about everything – but I haven't the time. Good thing isn't it?! How I long for the day when you and I will be together in our own home and independent of everyone else. It's very hard to be patient about everything.

Barely a week later she was even more depressed as Dad's unit was suddenly whisked away to Southampton.

17.5.44

[…] I'm finding this the hardest time we have ever lived through. You seem so cut off and far away. It's so hard to find you in the letters you are obliged to write now. Sometimes I just don't know how to go on. But then I suppose you feel the same too. How many more years of our life have we to waste like this?

[…] I'm sorry this is such a gloomy letter but I feel weary, weary. And as seems inevitable with me these days when I'm tired, I'm terribly depressed. I'm afraid of what the invasion of Europe is going to mean in horror and suffering for everyone else and for us – and our children. Worried because I don't know where on earth I'm going when there ceases to be room for me here. And so sick at heart because I am away from you and I do want and need you so much. Oh Darling, I do feel such a wretched woman to write to you like this when you have difficulty in keeping cheerful yourself. Forgive me Darling.

We children were, fortunately, just the distraction she needed, and Dad obviously delighted in news of our progress, judging by the detailed information of our every breath. It was a blessing too that she so loved the countryside and could write at the end of even such a letter as this: *The cuckoos have been busy here too. We've had a good deal of rain yesterday and today and not before it was needed. It doesn't stop the joyous singing of the birds.*

My new cousin, Hilary, arrived at the end of May, which means that Twink was in hospital for two weeks or so and Mum was left in charge. *It has been about the busiest week of my life I think and that's saying something. As you know [...] I've had to cope with 4 children, run the house and look after Alan. Phew!! What a job it's all been.* She rose to the occasion well but looked forward to Nan's coming – she'd been granted permission to visit on compassionate grounds.

Family visits weren't always so readily allowed, since that part of Dorset was a so-called 'restricted area'. Indeed, at Easter that year, when Mu was spending a few days with them, the village policeman arrived and ordered her to leave for 'official reasons'. They were all alarmed, disappointed then indignant to be told that she was not closely enough related and neither had she sufficiently important business to permit her to stay.

Once he moved to Southampton, Dad had to be careful to carry proof of both his and Mum's identities and address when he visited, as papers were rigorously checked at Dorchester station. However, Dad's travels and, therefore visits were, in any case, severely curtailed by an embargo on journeys beyond a twenty-five mile radius of the camp. It led them to toy briefly with thoughts of renting a place within the Southampton area.

4.5.44

It's just one blow after another for us now, isn't it? I suppose one day it will come right – but just which day I wonder. I'm getting to a stage where I just feel numb inside and half the time, I can't feel anything at all. That's alright if only I could be like it all the time but sometimes the strain is too much and I feel utterly wretched and miserable. But I shouldn't be writing all this. I expect you experience similar feelings and when all's said and done I'm only one of millions of women who are forced to suffer – and my suffering isn't, I suppose, anything like that of some. But all this suffering business is comparative, isn't it?

Depression and guilt settled firmly on her for the next few weeks. She felt guilty that demands at home prevented her from writing daily, guilty when she did write at burdening him with her despair, guilty too for feeling so despairing: *I wish I could rise above everything – but I'm not one of those clear-souled people.* There was even greater guilt when she compared her situation with the thousands of women whose husbands were fighting and the many widows.

So far, there had been no response to the advert for housing they had placed in the *Methodist Recorder*, and Mum wondered gloomily whether it had anything to do with the fact of mentioning that Dad was in the Non-Combatant Corps...*as I thought we might as well be ourselves at the outset.* Dad suggested that he should take a long leave and go house-hunting himself, but Mum couldn't bear the thought of this leave being tagged on to the end of his service – whenever that might be. She increasingly missed his physical presence.

Her depression lifted occasionally but now she felt more anxiety, as Hilary would soon need the cot which I was occupying. Naturally, Dad was very worried about her and about the increasing stresses within the little house at Evershot. He well understood her words: *There are too many of us trying to live under the same small roof and we each have too much to do and get easily tried because we are tired.* He was aware too of the clash of personalities involved, and felt deeply frustrated by his inability to do anything constructive to help. As the weeks passed he missed my brother and me, and feared that Peter in particular would forget him. Along with the regular parcels of clothes to be washed – did you really do all his washing, Mum? – Dad included sweets from his sweet ration especially for Peter. Mum, for her part, sprinkled even the most heartbreaking letters with anecdotes of our progress. There are many which served to reassure him that he was not forgotten: *Peter asked me to tell him a story about Daddy so I told him about you sitting at your desk writing and then going to the petrol pump and putting petrol in a big lorry. He's always asking me to tell him the story again and this morning when he passed the petrol pumps by Christopher's at the bottom of the hill, he said, "That's what Daddy does." Oh, I've just remembered – Peter put his finger in his mouth and flipped it along his cheek hoping to make a 'pop' when he moved his finger. He said, "Daddy does that!" – You know how you make a popping noise – so you see, he does remember you and not just someone about whom Mummy often speaks...*

I can't help but compare Peter's situation with that of the many children who didn't have the chance to see their fathers for years and then faced huge problems when these strange men re-entered their lives after the war. Nonetheless, as I read these daily letters I found myself feeling ridiculously tense and worried about the overcrowding of the house and the increasing pain of separation. I became caught up in my babyhood progress and grew quite proud of my brother's prowess. Even the minutiae of Dad's laundry were captivating as I followed the march of lost socks and pyjama mending and understood how important it was for Mum to feel she was doing *something* for him. Most worrying was the desperate hunt for a house; not a letter passed without some reference to a home of their own. I minded, as each attempt seemed to lead nowhere.

Suddenly, out of the blue, Dad received a telegram:

2.8.44

Every possibility cottage rent here confirming Wednesday = Phyll

How you must have cheered with relief, Dad. I certainly did. Stupid, really, since I know very well what happened. The promised details followed and unleashed a long-submerged side of Mum's character as she planned and organised. There was a breathlessness and vigour about her which was new.

4.5.44

My Beloved,

    I must write to you about the first real home of our own we are to have. The cottage is the one attached to the forge and has a decent sized garden which has an exit to the lane at the back. It won't seem too cramped to Peter after the big one here. There are two decent sized bedrooms, the ceilings of which slope in places rather like the end and middle bedrooms at Wilcott Manor and the windows are small and almost ground level like those too. However, they aren't bad. They lead out of one another. There is a large landing with a window and a funny recess and at a pinch a single bed could be put up and the whole curtained off in an emergency. Downstairs there is a tiny sitting room on the right of the front door and a good-sized kitchen on the left with a range in good order. The stairs lead out of the kitchen and there is a pantry in it and a good space with a window where the pram can go when not in use. The passage leads into a sizeable scullery with copper and sink and draining board. I should like to try and get an electric cooker if you approve. It would mean buying it I'm afraid, but it is so inconvenient to have to rely on fire cooking and the fuel ration is too little really. The bucket lavatory is outside of course. The cottage is let to us for 7/6 a week and rates which amount to about £1-16-8 each 2 year and are paid up to September. Isn't it amazing? Mr Wheller [the blacksmith] *wants me to sign an agreement and I'd rather do so as it's much more satisfactory but it's not ready yet. He's going to try and get some distempering done for us by the Estate painter [...] I'll try and draw a rough plan but it's very rough as I'm not much good at it! [...] I'm so glad to think we have got somewhere at last and now, of course, impatient to get the furniture from Croydon.*

She continued by detailing each long-stored piece and planning where it would go, down to the last strip of linoleum.

From the depths of gloom Mum was transported into a hive of activity, and no unexpected difficulties cropped up to ruin her delight and enthusiasm. I wondered, as I read, how on earth all the bits and pieces could be brought from Croydon. Magically, this presented no difficulties, since a Mr Legg in the village took cattle up to London each week and was willing to make a detour to Croydon for their belongings. Would the cattle lorry be in a fit state to carry furniture after housing cows all the way up to London? Mum didn't seem bothered. In fact, her only doubts concerned her mother-in-law: *you'll understand when I say I hope your mother doesn't offer to come and help me put things straight – she'd be too keen to do it her way and I _do_ want it _our_ way! What a pig I am!* It's all right, Mum – I sympathise with you; you and Dad had been married for four years and this was your first opportunity to enjoy a place of your own. I hope Dad didn't find it too difficult to dissuade his mother from coming. She certainly offered, and he would have been uncomfortable about putting her off. Mum had to encourage him to sweeten her a little.

The ecstasies over Forge Cottage were soon overtaken by plans for the garden: *[It] is larger than I realised and has considerable possibility. There is room for winter greens and for grass and flowers, so Peter won't find his activities too much curtailed. It's a reasonably private garden too, being bounded on one side by the extremities of the Rectory garden, which is huge, and on the other side by a fairly high box hedge beyond which is Mr Wheller's garden.* At last, she sounded settled and delighted to plan for a certain future.

Her joy and enthusiasm almost tripped her up as information about the cottage, news and love tumbled chaotically from her pen and she told of her father's short visit: *Daddy likes the cottage and wouldn't mind retiring there! He's serious.*

The sparkling mood continued after she had moved in, despite rare visits from Dad. It was so much more relaxing to decide for herself how she'd organise her daily life around us children, and at last she felt secure. Mr Wheller, the blacksmith and landlord, continued to be on very good terms with her, and his wife looked in on us from time to time.

In late September, Dad delighted her still further by managing to acquire a sewing machine – no mean achievement in the war years.

27.9.44

My Beloved

Everything is happening this week. Yesterday the fuse box for the cooker came, then the cooker arrived. After that the coalman came – I was almost entirely left with only coal dust. We all went 'wooding' before tea and on our return Mr Wheller walked in with 4 nice chickens – Rhode Island Reds – so far 3 eggs!!! He paid 10/- each for them – a bargain isn't it? Then this morning your letter came announcing about the sewing machine. Oh Darling, I am thrilled.

Nan had infected Mum with some of her enthusiasm for sewing, if not her flair, and she made most of our clothes by hand. The machine made a considerable difference to the scope of her needlework and opened the doors to far more ambitious creations once precious materials became available.

Dad's visits were few and far between but sufficient for them to dig and roll an area for grass and to plant vegetables and flowers, just as Mum had planned. Peter loved having Dad there but was understandably jealous of Mum's attentions, and sometimes retreated under the dining table to sulk. There was no problem about getting him out again – they only had to put their arms round each other for him to catapult out to join in the cuddle.

Even Mum's tales of Peter missing Dad seemed less anguished now: *I had a queer night with Peter on Sunday. He woke between 9.30 and 10pm and sobbed and fretted and didn't seem able to know what was the matter. This went on till well after midnight and he was restless in his sleep. However, he slept on till about 7.30am and didn't seem the least put out during the day. I don't know what was the cause, but wondered if it was because you were going[had gone?]. You mean a good deal to him now and he talks about you so much, bless him! [...] I forgot to tell you that the other day Peter, Hazel and I were going along Park Lane and Peter was holding my hand. Then he put up his other hand and said, "If Daddy were here, I could hold his hand this side." Oh Darling, the tears often spring to my eyes when he says things like that. To think that now we have a little son who misses you.*

At her birthday in October that year, Mum was highly amused and touched to receive good wishes from a number of Dad's colleagues, including one in verse from his very good friend Potts. I remember Dad telling us that Potts was a dab hand at rhyming couplets and even managed to persuade extra leave out of their superiors with these lines:

> Sir, will you graciously grant
> Leave – for the death of my aunt.
> You cannot believe
> How much 'twould relieve my feelings –
> But don't if you can't!

There was from Dad no birthday visit, but a letter to which she responds with longing and a calmness that had been absent for many months. It had been a long time since her knight in shining armour had carried her off – but perhaps there would be a happily ever after.

Forge Cottage

For the whole of the next year Mum's life revolved happily around us and Forge Cottage. Her letters were full of visits from friends and relatives and happily shared meals with Twink and Alan and the children, or picnics on her own lawn. She walked the lanes with us and gloried in the wild flowers which she could now name with ease.

The sewing machine was put to good use and her letters went into loving detail about garments which were under the needle and plans for further dungarees, blouses and so on. When both the iron and the sewing machine begin to play up, and then the cooker, I expected her to be plunged into despair. Instead, she was simply cross – and added another explanation for her more placid outlook: *This is indeed a much easier stage with the infants and I find I'm not in quite such a hectic rush all day. Consequently, of course, my temper isn't so easily ruffled.*

In late October she received a parcel from one of Dad's Guernsey relatives, who had been evacuated to Scotland with her grandson. It contained many very useful items of clothing and shoes for Pete.

She had happy stories of Peter to report: *Peter "wrote" a letter to you this evening but unfortunately tore it up. He was telling you that he can wash his own hands now! He is so proud of the fact and really does it very well […] and he likes to have a drink from the tap while he's doing it when he gets ready for dinner! "Like pussy does," he says, for there's a picture in one of his books of a pussy drinking at the tap. He grows lovelier every day and is most helpful in many ways. I wish I didn't sometimes get irritable with him. I love him so much and he gives me such joy. He talks so much about you.*

Mummy sent me a potato masher and I use it for mashing the chickens' food. The other day after dinner Peter said, "I'll do this, (mash the food) and you get on with the washing up, dear old thing"!! I don't know __what__ made him call me that! Now it is his daily job to mash the chickens' food while I wash up.

Prayers were obviously said at bedtime, and Peter's curiosity about God and church led Mum to take him to the Brethren Chapel. This was, presumably, rather like the Quakers, as the service was largely silent and was punctuated by Peter's rather piercing remarks. I am amazed that she thought this suitable for a two-and-a-half-year-old and, unsurprisingly, he cried after a while and they departed, picking me up in the pram outside. She was so naïve and tense about her Christianity yet was always so relaxed about other things – the human body for example. Poor Dad wasn't so sure: *I'm vastly amused to find that your small son embarrasses you when he makes remarks about your person! – I'm wondering when I'll ever be allowed to perform my toilet in private again!*

This reminds me of another story about Pete from this time. Mum had taken him into the village church to see the flowers arranged for a special occasion, and Pete looked with interest at the display. He stood gazing for quite a while at some particularly exotic blooms, then pointed at a long, furled bud and said, in the carrying tones of a small child, "It's like a penis!" Mum agreed, but had a hard time composing her features to meet the scandalised eyes of the other adults there.

Dad obviously loved hearing of Peter's latest exploits, and was amused to hear that he had *some imaginary "little boys" and he talks away to them. They come to meals too, but are apt to be a bit of a nuisance as they have to have chairs put for them to sit on!!*

She was cheered by a lovely letter from her father-in-law which boosted her often-flagging confidence in being a mother. It also contained an invitation to spend some time in Croydon. However, she felt that the problems of raising the fare and organising care of the hens, not to mention the dangers of V2s, outweighed the benefits of seeing family. She also feared that coming back to live alone again after the visit would be too hard.

At the beginning of 1945 Mum's life seemed more sociable. She writes of visits exchanged with local women, wives of Dad's army friends – and, of course, to Twink. She was obviously accepted in the village now despite Dad's non-combatant status.

Tonight Mrs Broadway (farmer's wife across the road) called and gave me an envelope for you. They had a whist drive and raffle to raise funds for presents for local men in the forces. I was quite overwhelmed that you'd been included and expressed much gratitude. It is decent of them, isn't it? There is 21/- in the envelope. I enclose the envelope and suggest you write to Mrs Broadway [...] I'll give you the cash when you come home, darling.

Peter is delighted with his wheelbarrow and ark and tells everyone about them. The darling – he is lovely. And you are so clever. [They must both have been made by Dad.]

Georgie managed to get away from Croydon and the shop, but his stay was all too short:

I've missed Daddy a lot since he went. [...]

Yes, 1944 was a year of many joys for us in spite of everything. Hazel Christine and our own home all in one year was a tremendous blessing.

I'm foolishly glad I was a blessing.

A few weeks later she had more company, as Muriel arrived. With her was Chris, the youngest of Dad's sisters, who'd been working as a land girl and was about to marry a Canadian soldier. In July she sent Dad a bubbly letter:

My very dear George (and Phyll),

My first instructions to you are – before you read another word of this stupendous and intoxicated epistle – to go and sit down somewhere with a glass of water and bottle of sal volatile within easy reach. Smelling salts and burnt feathers would probably be also beneficial, to say nothing of an attractive V.A.D. here and there, just to take your temperature and loosen your corsets or other constricting garment (He's fainted!) [...] Well, brother and sis, what are your reactions? Surprised? Shocked? Amused? Dumbfounded? [...]

We decided we'd better talk to Dad this weekend and find out his reactions. After dinner, when all the women folk were engaged upon the washing up and Dad was meditating on his sermon, Chad thought he should take the bull by the horns and beard the lion in his den while the sun shone. I wished him luck and dispatched him to his mission. [...] I ventured into the hall, but the study door was firmly closed. [...] I went into the drawing room and tried to read, but found myself concentrating on the mumble of voices next door. Then I tried playing the piano. I played "Ich liebe dich" by Grieg – just to give him moral support. Then the study door opened and Dad came out into the hall. "Mam," he said in authoritative tones. Mother obediently trotted out of the dining room and once more the study door shut firmly. Then I tried "Hear my prayer" with the loud pedal on, in case Dad was offering firm resistance. I hoped he could hear my prayer in the study sufficiently well not to ask me in too – I knew I would have hysterics if he did. However, after about a week, the door opened again, then the drawing room door opened, and Chad came in looking something between a boiled beetroot and a Turner sunset. My first reactions were that Dad had given him a thorough dressing down and forbidden him to enter these portals again. I hardly dared ask him how he got on – but I didn't really need to. His first remark was, "Well, I guess we're engaged." Curtain.

Much love to you both,
Slightly intoxicatedly,
Chris

I'm not surprised Mum enjoyed their company, given her closeness to Muriel – and Chris's sparkling character must have been such a change. They were both very good with the children, and their visit was swiftly followed by one from Dad's younger brother, John. Shortly after, she writes: *I was yesterday complimented about my French accent by an Italian prisoner! Two of them were walking towards the village when Mu and I returned home with the children after seeing Chris off at the station. One picked some flowers and made a bunch for Hazel. They asked, "Parlez-vous français?" And I sputtered out a few remarks and they chatted a bit on the way, asking about the children and mon mari (husband, in case you've forgotten!). "Il est à la guerre?" Anyway, to cut a long story short, one of them asked, "Vous allez promener ce soir?" But Madame replied firmly, "non"!!!! So much for international co-operation!!*

By May Dad had moved yet again, this time to Wells. Despite the end of the war, Mum was beset by depression once more, both on a personal level and on a wider scale as news filtered through of what our victory meant for the defeated: *it does bring me unlimited joy to know that your time in the army is definitely nearing its end, but somehow this week problems both international and personal seem to weigh heavily upon me.* [The British had taken Lübeck and Wisman on the Baltic coast, and Canadian units Oldenburg just a few days before.] *The wretched business about Mussolini and the lady, and the San*

Francisco bickerings all serve to make me wonder just what sort of a world we're in now.

[The references to *Mussolini and the lady* relate to the execution of Mussolini and his mistress near Lake Como on 28th April. And the *San Francisco bickerings* were the month-long discussions which resulted in the drawing up of a constitution for the United Nations – something I would have expected Mum to approve of.]

A few days later, she writes: *Mr Bevin's speech is most disappointing.* [He warned of the impossibility of demobbing all soldiers at once and flooding a non-existent job market. There was also the problem of rebuilding housing.] *I had been foolish enough to think (with many other people) that we'd be able to form <u>some</u> idea of the time when you'll come home for good. The thought of possibly the best part of another year is almost unbearable.*

Dad's third sister, Joyce, was by now in Germany with a Quaker relief team, one of the first groups of civilians to enter Belsen. Mum had seen a copy of Joyce's first letter from there, but it might as well have been from Birmingham for all the attention she gave it. Why didn't she cry out in horror at the atrocities? But I realise from reading some of Joyce's letters myself that censorship forbade much detail. It would be a long time before the world knew the half of what went on at Belsen and in other concentration camps.

'Belsen' reverberates in my head, and I have to read the next letter excerpt twice before I can take in its relative triviality.

I've done quite a bit in the garden today – putting the pea sticks in and hosing a bit and also hand weeding part of the potato patch. The weeds have spread all over it after the spell of wet weather. It has been a glorious day today. Tomorrow if the weather holds, Twink and co. are all coming for a picnic tea on the lawn which has also incidentally benefited from the recent rain.

I'm glad that, for the moment, they are all protected from the horrors and wickedness that will soon become common knowledge. By the time news of these was released, Mum and Dad would be reunited and better able to bear it. Meantime it was her own little world that was important. The only way she managed to survive was by blotting out almost everything that wasn't directly her concern. She wasn't unsympathetic – far from it – but without Dad she was, unfortunately, not strong enough to shoulder any of the world's burdens or guilt.

So I read in her letters of Hazel cutting more teeth and learning to walk, which seemed to make Pete revert to babyhood. She wrote of Dad's cold and his short leave in Croydon, looking for somewhere to live. There was bad news from Guernsey concerning the property owned by Dad's parents. Much of what they treasured had been destroyed or requisitioned by the Germans during the Occupation. However, there was pleasure too, as Chris had by now married Chad, and Mu had seen the photos.

Mu says the wedding photos are good and Edward [a friend from Ghana] *says that I am, in appearance, his ideal of an English woman!!! Needless to say, I'm highly flattered!! – I am but frail and human, darling!*

As May progressed, Mum was delighted to welcome Dad's cousin Dorothy and her two small children. Her practical side was reasserting itself:

Can you work out as near as possible just what money you'll get when you leave the army? I've been thinking that if we do get the chance of a house, we might be glad to borrow privately from someone with that money as security. I wish I could feel there was some hope of letting this place furnished at say £2.2.0. a week [Does she mean *a month*? Her rent is only 7/6 a week] *for perhaps 3 or 6 months whilst I go to Croydon for the winter to try to get us somewhere to live. It would be a chance to put a little by in the bank as well as knowing things here would be alright.*

Plans for the garden proceeded despite all the talk of returning to Croydon. When Vernon, Dorothy's husband, joined them for a few days, they all set to and planted out vegetables and tomatoes.

In July, Mum took us children to Croydon for a week or two, and Dad had a few days leave there too.

16.7.45

My dearest one,

I do hope you got back safe and without difficulty on Sunday morning. I wonder how much of the thunder storm you witnessed. It was terrific and lasted till far into the small hours.

I know you will have been thinking of us today and be glad to know that we arrived back here safely just after 5pm. It was well on time too. Hazel was very fretty and miserable almost the whole journey. She's sound asleep now. Twink and Alan were waiting our arrival. Twink had put flowers everywhere and set tea and made it for us. She had also bottled four jars of raspberries and done various bits of washing and ironed a few oddments I'd left – isn't she a gem!

The weeds in the garden are legion again even after such a short absence. I suppose the rain has helped.

Peter visited his old haunts in the garden and set to work at once hoeing and clipping with the shears! He also brought the eggs in. However, before all this he did find time to put out his engines and signal the very minute we got home.

Suddenly I'm at a loss for details as Dad didn't keep all of the letters. However, it was plain that they had decided that Mum should leave Evershot permanently and move into 169 with Nan and Georgie. Dad was lucky that he had a job to go back to in Croydon, so it seemed logical for Mum to be on the spot to look out for somewhere to live once the army let him go. Once more the furniture was to be stowed away in the obliging Mr Legg's cattle truck – easier now since mileage and petrol restrictions for removals had been lifted.

There are no more letters from Evershot. Did she have any regrets about leaving there? I can't imagine choosing to go to Croydon after living in such an idyllic place. But of course I'm missing the main point. At long last they were on the brink of starting a life truly together, and that was the most important thing of all.

By Mum's birthday in October Dad had moved again, this time to Ilminster.

15.10.45
169 Davidson Road

Peter was thrilled when he learnt this morning that it is my birthday. He said at once, "Has your cake got icing on it?" So, of course, I had to make a cake – a chocolate one. At tea time Peter kept saying to me, "I <u>have</u> enjoyed your birthday, Mummy!"

Hazel is being very mummyish. She says more and more. When I put on my new jumper after tea she said, "I do like it." She's being rather a scamp at bed time and the last two evenings I've left her to cry it out. Poor lamb! But she <u>is</u> a pickle.

They were both delighted to put pennies in the slot and make a toy caged bird sing at Allders [a department store]. *They had 4 pennyworth! Peter insisted on our coming down in the lift and was very irate when I wouldn't go up again in it.*

The other day he asked me if we heard God speak and I tried to explain about listening and thinking and then understanding what God wanted us to do. Tonight at prayers, when we were thinking about friends and my birthday, Peter suddenly said, "When is God's birthday?" So I said I wasn't sure. At once he replied, "You just be quiet, Mummy and then you'll know." I did as I was told but couldn't for the life of me think what to say, so I said I'd have another think about it and tell him another time. It has since occurred to me that I might have said Christmas time. That may confuse him least of all answers […] Oh that I had the wisdom of Solomon!

Goodnight my Beloved and God bless you. I love you so – your own Phyll

20.10.45

My Beloved

It is very late but I must write to you tonight or I'll miss the Sunday post.

Daddy (Georgie) is in bed suffering from pleurisy. He looks ghastly and is in pain all the time and breathing noisily. He had a cold too, and seemed to go through similar stages as the rest of us but on Thursday night he seemed a bit off colour and on Friday morning was very poorly. He felt he must go to the shop and see about various things but came home mid-morning and has been in bed ever since. It is very worrying and I hope to heaven he doesn't get worse. […] You can tell how poorly Daddy is as he let me wash him this morning.

Oh, how I wish you were here – I feel so much more complete when you are with me and I know I could cope better with everything. You do help to steady me. Nights have been so disturbed with Hazel for so long and she's been difficult during the day – and now this – I'm getting so bad-tempered with our darling children and don't seem able to help myself. They are so lovely too. I ought to be able to keep my patience when they are being so difficult […] why on earth don't the people in the war office let us live our own lives. It's so long we're waiting on their pleasure. So sorry your work is further complicated by so many comings and goings. Poor you! I should hate it.

Last Sunday when we were in the dining-room Peter turned off the light and in the flickering firelight he got so thrilled and said it was like Christmas. He had to show Nanny and Georgie what it was like when they subsequently came into the room. Dear little fellow, he must have dreamt of you the other morning for when he woke up, he asked, "Is my Daddy here?" He seems to understand when I said he must have had a dream about you.

Mum remained at Nan and Georgie's for several months, but by April Dad's parents were planning a long trip to Guernsey and suggested she might like to move to their house with us children. She would have Mu as company as well as Chris, who was impatiently waiting to go to Canada to and rejoin Chad.

I don't know what to say about our sojourn at Fermain. [The house name – also referred to as '88'.] *I can see the point about dashing off to visit a house at a moment's notice, but somehow can't imagine that contingency arising. Maybe I'm pessimistic! I'm not sure that you are right – I mean your mother would be disappointed if we didn't stay on after they come back from Guernsey.*

Peter amused me at tea-time. He had tried the experiment of sweetening his milk with a little jam left on his plate and some sultanas out of his cake. Having drunk the milk, he said his cup smelt nasty and asked if he could wash it. On getting up to do so, he said, "We don't want a nasty smell hanging about the place, do we?"

I love you so very much. God bless and keep you dearest. [...]

P.S. Hazel has several repair jobs for Daddy "when he comes home from 'Minster"!! [Ilminster]

But Dad didn't come home from *'Minster* as the army moved him yet again, this time to Taunton. Even his patience was wearing thin by now. There was still no date for his release. He persuaded Mum to move to Fermain, his parents' house in Croydon, and as if by magic, they heard of a house. Georgie's contacts in the shop had at long last led them to a small terraced property in Wallington, just a few miles from Croydon. It would be an easy bike ride for Dad when he was at last able to take up his job again.

23.4.46
88 Chatsworth Road

My Beloved,
*   Mrs Miles has been into the shop and says that so far as she knows*
the rent for 18, Bute Road is 35/- weekly, a 3yrs agreement being
required. The house is now vacant and workmen are doing necessary
repairs. [A bomb fell at the entrance to Beddington Park just
down the road and caused some minor damage to the terrace.]
Isn't it marvellous? Really it all seems to be fitting together as a jig-saw
puzzle. I didn't at one stage imagine it possible that we would have a
house of our <u>own</u> to go to when you came out of the army. It may be
a small place and a high rental, but it is a house and <u>we</u> together will
make it our HOME!

There are no more letters – but ten days later Dad was demobbed. His
Soldier's Release Book is beside me on the desk, and I read with pleasure and
no surprise: "Military conduct: Exemplary", and the additional testimonial:
"Very capable, sober and hard-working. He has held a very responsible
position in this unit office, which he has filled most satisfactorily. Strongly
recommend for any responsible position of trust." It seems so little to sum up
five years.

My conscious life began here with the move to Bute Road. I remember
so much there: the army blankets, instead of a carpet, on the dining room
floor; a marble-topped washstand in the kitchen as a cupboard and work
surface. This was a good height for perching children on to do up shoes and
leggings – but the icy marble was so chilly on my bottom. In the bathroom
was a magnificent geyser, all polished copper and rather alarming. But more
important than the physical memories was the feeling of security. Each day
had a rhythm to it, with Dad cycling home at dinner time and again at
teatime – every day. No more "Daddy one day" but Daddy there always.
What kissing and hugging there was at each arrival and departure. Even
Mum could now smile when she said goodbye.

Meta's war

Stockrend, January 23rd
1947

My dear Mrs Shaw,

I wonder, if I shall ever get a connexion with you and your dear Phyllis after so many years. I send this letter only to let you know, that I am still alive after so many "travellings" through Germany and now in Sweden. I don't remember any other address in England, I don't know anything about Phyllis, and Mr. Parkinson, and Mr. Shaw. I should like to know all about you and your family.

I am in Sweden with my husband and three children. My mother-in-law and my sister-in-law are also here.

If you ever recieve this letter, please do answer me as quickly as possible. Then I shall write to you more about my "travellings".

Many greetings to Mr. Shaw, Phyllis, and to all my old friends in London.

Yours affectionate
Meta Lender - Tonkman

My address:
Mr. Lender
Donnerstigen 5 c/o Pettrsson Stocksand, Sweden

Meta's letters travelled with Mum throughout the war. She re-read them once or twice and felt immeasurably sad when all hope of contact was lost. In her head she told Meta many things in an intermittent, one-sided dialogue, and she grieved for her lost friend and the loss of friendship.

Then one day, out of the blue, came this:

23.1.47
Stocksund, Sweden

My dear Mrs Shaw,
I wonder if I shall ever get a connexion with you and your dear Phyllis after so many years. I send this letter only to let you know, that I am still alive after so many "travellings" through Germany and now in Sweden. I don't remember any other address in England. I don't know anything about Phyllis and Mr Parkinson, and Mr Shaw. I should like to know all about you and your family.
I am in Sweden with my husband and three children. My mother-in-law and my sister-in-law are also here.
If you ever receive this letter, please DO answer me as quickly as possible. Then I shall write you more about my "travellings".
Many greetings to Mr Shaw, Phyllis, and to all my old friends in London.
Yours affectionately,
Meta Lender-Tonkman

I remember this letter arriving. Nan rushed it to Dad at the office and he cycled home with it at lunchtime. I didn't understand what was going on but clearly remember Mum bursting into tears and Dad taking her on his lap, sitting her on his knee to comfort her. It was all very worrying and confusing, especially since she kept saying how happy she was. I know I cried too and it all ended up with a rather damp family hug. Pete went back for afternoon school and Dad pedalled back to work, leaving me with Mum. We sat down together, so close and comfortable, and she told me the story of Meta and their friendship, of Meta's stay at 169 with her and Nan and Georgie and of Mum's visit to Estonia. I learned just a little about what war meant and met the word 'refugee' for the first time.

*

That afternoon was special. It involved just the two of us and seems to me to mark the beginning of my relationship with my mother as a separate person. It also fired my imagination about Meta and her family. Is that where this book really began?

Mum must have written at once to Meta, and she soon received the following reply:

5.2.47
Stocksund, Sweden

My dear, dear Phyllis,

Many thanks for your letter. I am so glad to have it. I am richer now to have you again after that I have lost almost all my relatives and friends. These years past have been hard for all nations in Europe. (Dear Phyllis, will you excuse my English. I have forgotten a lot of it. I haven't had any practice for years and I have had to speak other foreign languages.)

Perhaps it will interest you if I tell you, what has happened to our dear Eesti [Estonia] and with my family. Naturally, as I have seen it.

It was in June 1940 when Russian troops occupied the three Baltic Republics – without any fight. In [the] following months most of our politicians were arrested and afterwards deported to Russia. All began to seem unsafe for every-one who wasn't a communist. All merchants had to give up their shops, all larger houses didn't belong to their owners, but to the communistic occupation. Many labourers, who had been working hard for their lives long – to have it lazier in old days, some had built houses, or had some money in banks – they were poorer as never before. Not only that – they were titled as enemies of labour people – for they were rich. Farmers, who had more land than 75 [or is it 15?] acres had to give it up and they were named "kulaks" – the enemies of a communistic state. Therefore my brother's shop was taken away and as he was a "labourer's enemy" – his land was taken also. My mother-in-law could not be a schoolmistress any more.

[The] Estonian Army was incorporated with the Red Army. Incorporation was "entirely voluntary". But these officers who didn't join with the Red Army were arrested and they have not been seen after that. Therefore my husband preferred to incorporate.

In December 1940 my first child, daughter, May (we write Mai) was born. In May 1941 my husband went with his regiment to Russia. Mai was only five months old when I was left alone. In June, just before the war broke out between Germany and Russia there were arrested and deported thousands of Estonians, only from Tallinn 10% of inhabitants. Those who were arrested were mostly our educated classes. My husband lost his brother and his sister Juta (unmarried) and his brother-in-law (Ilka's husband). I myself – my father.

In the midst of the night the Russian soldiers knocked at the door and men and women, old people and small children had to leave their homes during some ten minutes taking only [a] few things with [them]. Lorries were standing before the houses and the journey into the unknown began. Goods trains were ready to bring these unhappy people to [the] East. And those people were treated a little bit worse than the cattle in Western Europe. They got neither drink nor eating and there was little place in the carriage to lie oneself rightly down. [...]

My brother and my mother-in-law – we were all saved by a miracle, as we were not at our homes that night. Days that followed were full of trouble, anguish and pain. Who would be the next ones? Therefore you can understand our joy when the war between Germany and Russia broke out. We saw through the war the only rescue. [...]

On these days I didn't know anything about Henno. My mother was in the country and I could not go there. I went with Mai (6 months old) to live in Nõmme (near Tallinn) to Henno's uncle, where I stayed till the end of August. When the German troops had occupied Tallinn, I went to live in my flat.

During the summer months our Estonian men were mobilised by the Russians and thousands of our men were not to be seen again. But there were also many, who hid themselves in [the] wood. So did my brother. When the German troops were there, they came out again and were free to live and to work in their own country. Perhaps you can't just understand us that we felt us free when there were German soldiers and German occupation. But when you have to choose between two evils, you prefer that one which hurts you less. The personal security was again guaranteed, if you were not a Jew, a communist or an active Estonian. In those days we had an opinion that this occupation was a preliminary one, and that the end of the war will bring freedom to all small nations.

Days passed and in October 1941 I got my first news of Henno, who was a prisoner of war in Germany. He had fled from the Red Army already in July. Life seemed a little lazier again. Henno came home in April 1942. He had lost a great deal of his weight (15 kg.); he had had a "good diet" in different prisoners' camps. (Many of his friends died from this "diet".)

Dear Phyllis, I shall end this time. There is just one thing I shall explain to you. Please don't write any letters to Estonia (Vaiknal) asking about my mother and my brother. It is not recommended in a communistic state to have connections with foreign countries. Your letter can make their lives only harder and cause their arrest (as it was in June 1941).

Excuse me if I don't answer your questions this time, but the following letters will explain you all.

Yours affectionately,

Meta.

P.S. I send you a photo of my children. Could you send me one of you and your children?

Mum, how on earth did you feel when you read this? I believe that your enormous sense of shame began here. You had suffered so much without Dad, but at least you knew where he was all the time. You knew he was safe. Did the problems of your war years suddenly seem unimportant? You had mentally acknowledged the suffering of so many war wives who didn't see their husbands for months or years at a time – or indeed ever again. But this was something so close to you and made personal the experiences which had hitherto only really touched you peripherally.

I've recently learned much more about Meta's wartime experience – many things that Mum never knew – and I find myself feeling glad she was spared some of these details. Why do I feel so protective? I think it's because I see now how Mum's ability to empathise with suffering could be self-destructive. As a child I used to watch her with apprehension when there was news on the wireless of earthquakes, floods, fires, war or domestic tragedy. Her face would stiffen and she'd close her eyes in horror as she imagined an individual caught up in the disaster. At such times I didn't dare speak to her or ask questions, as she seemed so consumed with pain and shrivelled into impotence. A bolder, more confident person might have rushed out and become involved with practical, cathartic things like the sort of well-orchestrated funds for food and clothing collections that are familiar to us today. But for Mum the grief and shared pain produced inaction and depression – and often guilt, because she was so lucky by comparison and didn't always acknowledge it.

There was quite enough in that February letter of Meta's to fill Mum's mind. I was moved by the clarity and deceptive simplicity and economy of expression when I first read it in 1987, although none of it was news to me. It was like flicking through a dimly remembered photo album and finding the images stunningly clear – and to those pictures I now have more to add.

I visualise Mrs Lender presiding over a meal, where her children are discussing the possibility of the Germans starting the war against the Russians. She knew some Russians when she was first married, for both her sister and husband had studied at St Petersburg. They were educated, aristocratic Russians with beautiful manners who spoke French and kissed her hand in a way that enchanted her. Into the debate she confidently tossed her own opinion: "I think the Russians are far superior to the Germans." There was a short silence before Uno, not long returned from a spell of work in the foreign office in Russia, quietly commented, "My dear mother, you don't know today's Russia." Meta, listening, felt her first real sensation of fear.

Her increasing fear is crystallized for me by another little episode when she went to visit an old schoolfriend. The apartment was very large, in a fine villa, and the rooms were sumptuously decorated and beautifully furnished. With growing horror, she learned that the Estonian boy her friend had married was a member of the communist underground, who'd been made a member of parliament by the Russians in one of their rigged elections – and that the flat had formerly belonged to a now deported minister. Meta desperately hoped that she'd concealed her own feelings as she listened to her friend being most emphatic that things would be better under the communists.

Terror came later. *There were arrested and deported thousands of Estonians.* One bright day in that June of 1941, Meta had an appointment with the dentist in Tallinn and decided to call on the Lender family before returning home.

She knew that Mrs Lender was in the country but expected to find Uno, Juta and Henno's younger sister, Ilka, with her little son, Peep. Peep's nanny opened the door. She said nothing, but frantically gestured for Meta to go away. For a moment Meta hesitated in confusion. Then she glimpsed Russian soldiers in the house and fled, terrified. She never saw Uno or Juta again.

A few days later Meta was approached by a tramp dressed in a filthy raincoat and cap, carrying a large paper parcel under his arm. She was startled at first, then recognised the face as one of Henno's friends. He told her that he was making his way to the country to hide, as his name was on the deportation list. The Lenders were on the list too. Ilka and Peep were safe because Ilka's married name was different – but Uno and Juta had been taken. *Who would be the next ones?*

Mrs Lender had, for the moment, avoided capture because she was in the country, but the Russians caught up with her not long afterwards. Along with many other Estonian deportees, she was loaded onto a boat in Tallinn harbour. But for some inexplicable reason – perhaps engine failure – the boat didn't depart at once. The delay was enough to save them all, as the German troops flooded into Tallinn and released them. They were more fortunate than some of the 23,000 Russian soldiers, civilians and deportees evacuated by sea from Tallinn harbour on 27th July – nearly half of whom drowned.

Perhaps you can't just understand us that we felt us free when there were German soldiers and German occupation. But when you have to choose between two evils, you prefer that one which hurts you less.

Henno too had chosen the lesser of two evils by leaving the Red Army at much the same time as his mother's miraculous escape. I haven't been able to discover quite where Henno was stationed on the miles of defensive border. Following Hitler's surprise attack on 22th June, the German army was swiftly a third of the way to Moscow from the German border; by the end of July it had made considerably more ground. At this point, Henno simply ran towards the German troops, risking the gunfire to give himself up. My most recent reading has shown me just how hazardous this was. Apart from the obvious danger of racing towards gunfire, there seems little evidence of German clemency towards prisoners from the eastern front. But Henno survived, and his identity as an unwilling Estonian conscript and not as a Red Army officer was eventually established and recognised.

In October 1941, as snow fell on the German army advancing into Russia, Meta received her first news that Henno was in Germany. By early

December the German army, ill-equipped against the intense cold and snow, was forced back from Moscow. For no particular detectable reason, Henno was allowed home in April 1942.

Just a month earlier in Oswestry my brother, Peter, was born, and Mum longed to share the news with Meta. She knew that Estonia had been occupied by the Russians then overtaken by Germany, and feared that Meta had died in the bombing raids on Tallinn.

Shortly after Pete's fifth birthday another long letter arrived from Sweden:

13.3.47
Stocksund, Sweden

My dear, dear Phyllis,

It is really a great pleasure to me to have your dear letter again. Your children are lovely! They look a great deal like you. And they have dark hair and dark eyes. My children are all fair and they have grey eyes – Ann's eyes are more blue. Your Peter has this month [a] birthday – many happy returns for his birthday. I am so glad that your children are better now and the weather is getting warmer, they can go out again. You must have it lovely to have your own home at last. I know that you have had a very severe winter this year, and you must have it very cold – I am afraid. Your houses are not built for such a cold weather, you have no stoves or central heatings in them. Oh, I dislike a cold unheated room.

Many thanks for your photo. I have none of them with me. Most of them I lost in Tallinn, where there was all burnt down, and others I left to my mother. I think you look like you did eight years ago. And you can smile as gay and lovely as before.

I am thankful to you, that you understand our sympathy to Germans. There are so different meanings and understandings. Your soldiers have fought against Germans with Russians, and our soldiers with Germans against Russians. In the beginning of German occupation it seemed impossible that the Russians could come back. We were not a free nation, but everyone could work and live, could have his house and land. We had again our flat for ourselves – during Russian time I had to share my kitchen with four other families, for there was allowed only one room for each family.

Henno didn't get regular work in a hospital after his return, but my brother helped us a great deal as well as my mother-in-law. In February 1943, Ann was born, and I was so happy to have another daughter. Then I didn't want a boy.

During this time there were so many Russian air raids over Tallinn and in March we had to leave our flat and go to live in Pirita. I didn't know that I left my home for ever. In August I went to live [with] my mother. My mother and brother were kind and helpful to me and to my children. Ann was my mother's dearest. In March 1944 there were again many air-raids over Tallinn and in one night half of Tallinn was bombarded and burnt down. This house where was my home, was burnt down as well. That was a great loss to me and Henno. Henno could not work any more in Tallinn. He was later on working in Haapsalu and Pärnu (do you remember these names?) in Estonian Legion hospitals.

[At Pärnu the Grand Hotel people wanted to put us all in the same room.]

In February 1944 Russian troops came over [the] Narva River and the Russian occupation stood again as a terrible monster before us. Estonian men were mobilized against Russians and they were fighting as Estonian units under German command. There were great fights near Narva and Tartu during spring and summer. We had much hope, but there was more hopelessness and fear until the end of September. It was 19th September when it was clear that all was over and the end was there. It came so suddenly, that the German army drew back from the front and we were left without defence against Russians.

Henno telephoned to me from Pärnu in good time. I had to pack my things during the night. My brother was not at home, and my mother did not want to come with us. She said she is too old and unwell to come to a foreign country. I couldn't persuade her to do otherwise she wanted. From [the] neighbourhood we got a man, who brought me and my children with few things to Pärnu. From my brother and my mother, I have not heard anything since that day. That drive was a long one – (80 klm.) Ann was only 19 months old and she didn't feel herself very well.

Henno's message came on 19th September 1944. They were already frightened by the reports on the wireless that the Russians were returning. How could Meta leave? There was no time to hesitate, no time to make careful decisions about what to take and what to abandon – and no time to consider what would happen to them all.

Meta didn't question Henno's decision to escape, but couldn't at first find anyone who was willing to take her south to meet him. Most of their friends and workers were too frightened of being cut off by the Russians, and preferred to stay where they were and take their chance under Russian domination again. Meta gathered her belongings together with mounting panic – but almost as she despaired of any help, one of her uncle's workers from Nõmme arrived in the yard with a horse and cart. He brushed aside her thanks for his kindness, saying he had little to lose by fleeing again as he was already a refugee from an area close to the Russian–Finnish–Estonian border.

They quickly packed the cart, and Meta climbed in with the two bewildered and fretful children. Saying goodbye to her mother was agonising. She was reminded of the dreadful separation when she first went to school in Tallinn – but this was far, far worse.

It was a jolting, uncomfortable journey and little Ann cried for much of the time, sensing something of the fear and urgency as they drove along. For the horse, eighty kilometres was a long way, and Meta was as aware as her driver that they couldn't afford to go too fast and overtire the animal. They arrived at the outskirts of Pärnu at last, but the relief was short-lived as the German guards wouldn't let them pass and wouldn't accept Meta's explanation that her husband was working at the military hospital. It crossed her mind that they should have brought food or something to use as a bribe, but they simply hadn't thought of it in their effort to get away as quickly as possible. For the sake of the children, Meta tried to stay calm and self-possessed, but inside she was fighting panic as she contemplated the possibility of having to go back. Eventually an official appeared who knew the arrangements Henno had made for Meta. She said goodbye to the man who had brought her on this first stage of her journey. She never found out what happened to him, but would always remember him as one of the kindest people in the world.

As Meta and the children were led to Henno's room at the hospital, she learned with horror that Henno had borrowed a car and rushed northwards to Tallinn, avoiding areas occupied by the Russian forces, to make his mother and Ilka leave on any boat they could find. She tried to concentrate on reassuring Ann and Mai and settled them down to rest. All the time she thought of her mother, her brother – and of Henno. What would happen if he didn't make it to Tallinn? Supposing he was overtaken by the advancing Russians and didn't reach Pärnu before the Germans withdrew? Should she escape anyway or stay and hope to have news of him? She was so exhausted emotionally and physically by the events of the past twenty-four hours that she slept a little. Some time later she was woken – by Henno – and for a little while it was enough that they were all together.

Meta explained to Henno that she'd been unable to persuade her mother to join them and that Erik, her brother, hadn't been at home when she left, and Henno, in turn, described his journey to Tallinn and the great difficulty he had had in making his mother realise the danger. She had become very religious since Uno and Juta were deported, and believed nothing would happen to her. She had twice miraculously escaped deportation by the Russians, so thought prayer would surely save her again. Henno didn't have the time for lengthy arguments. He was desperate to get back to Pärnu, hoping to find Meta there, and finally convinced Mrs Lender that she and Ilka should leave.

21st September we left Pärnu (with many of the wounded from Henno's regiment and a few other families) on a ship to reach Germany. We wanted to go to Sweden, but there was no possibility for us, and Henno had to do his duty against wounded soldiers in the hospital. Mrs Lender and Ilka with Peep went from Tallinn to Sweden. During these voyages very many ships were wrecked. The Russians were bombing all the time and the sea was very rough. Our ship reached Gotenhafen [Gdynia?] *happily.*

On 25th August 1944 Tartu, where Mum had signed her name in the university library visitors' book in 1939, fell to the Soviets – and Tallinn fell some days later. By 13th October all three Baltic States were in Russian hands. Three days earlier Churchill told Stalin that the Western Allies wanted every country to have "the form of government which its people desire"...

In Germany we have been living in different places and twice we had to escape from the Russians. And twice I have been sitting with my children the whole night through. Two months we lived in Zoppot (near Danzig) [Sopot, near Gdansk], *then Kühlingsborn (near Rostock)* [about 280 miles further west]. *There have been always other Estonians and I haven't been just alone. In the end of April 1945* [at much the same time as Joyce, Dad's sister, entered Bergen-Belsen with the Quaker relief team] *we had to leave Kühlingsborn in a hurry and we left many of our few things behind. I got a place in a lorry for my children and myself. Henno had to come on foot. We thought that the west Allies would come to Mecklenburg – therefore we had to fly in the last moment. This drive was very unpleasant – it was into the unknown and there were so many air-raids on the roads. In Eutin (in Schleswig-Holstein from Lübeck 30 klm west) I stood at night in the street and waited for morning light to find lodging for us. The only thought has been not to fall into Russian hands and now the British troops were in Lübeck and that meant for us to live again.*

The flight from Kühlingsborn was terrifying, with air raids raging incessantly close by. Meta felt more frightened and alone than at any other time. She held Mai and Ann close, unable to stop Ann's constant crying, conscious of the other frightened bodies wedged close to her in the crowded lorry, and remembered her flight from Estonia in the horse-drawn cart. This journey was even worse. At Eutin the vehicle stopped to set her down with her two small children and her two cases. An elderly woman got off too with her mentally disabled son, and they shuffled off to find lodgings. Meta sat down in the deserted street, wondering what on earth she should do. She had the address of an Estonian family a few miles away, which was why she had been dropped here – but how would she find the place? In any case, she couldn't think how to get the children there; at two and four years old they were unable to walk far, and she had the cases to carry. She settled the children down on a blanket on the ground and dozed fitfully herself, numbed into total inactivity by fear, sadness and sheer exhaustion. She was awoken while it was still dark by a voice saying, "Why are you sitting here?" She opened her eyes to see the concerned and friendly face of a man – "the kindest man in the whole world," she would say later. Quite where he had come from and what he was doing on his bicycle in the middle of the night Meta never knew, but he was more than willing to ride off to the address that she had, to give the occupants a note.

Before daybreak she was alarmed by the sound of vehicles moving, but fortunately it was retreating German troops and not Russian. As it grew light, Mr Toomse, her Estonian contact, came to find her. "The kindest man in the whole world" had delivered her note and described where she was. Mr Toomse couldn't provide any transport, but suggested that she should try to get a lift from one of the passing army vehicles. It seemed to her a ludicrous idea at first but, amazingly, she quickly found a willing driver, and later that day she was again met by Mr Toomse at a place he had suggested. He had arrived by bicycle and so was there well before her, since the army convoy moved very slowly. He took her to the authorities in the village and she was soon installed on the floor of a village schoolroom, along with about thirty other refugees. At last she and the children could sleep, but Meta was too anxious about Henno's safety to relax for long. Miraculously he joined them there, having made his way from Kühlingsborn to the Toomses' on foot. He had long since strategically shed both his uniform and army papers.

During Hitler's time in Germany we have days where there was cold and little to eat, but it wasn't too bad. After the flight from Kühlingsborn we lived in a small village [Büjendorf] near Eutin three months. In the country it was better food. We got enough milk for the whole family and country people are always more helpful especially in Germany when there are small children. We had a room – that was a carpenter's workroom with stone floor and a tiny kitchen range in it. But it was summer and the children were much out of doors. The village was full of refugees from East and capitulated soldiers.

In August 1945 we had to go to live in Lübeck in DP [displaced persons] *camp. During these months until March 1946 when British Mil-Gar and UNRRA* [United Nations Relief and Rehabilitation Administration] *took care of all Baltic refugees, we suffered neither cold nor hunger.*

A kindly British officer gave Meta chocolate for the children, but they'd never tasted chocolate before and didn't like it at all – so Meta ate it herself and found it perfectly delicious.

Later on the food wasn't a very good one, but I had saved a great deal from winter. In May 1946 we came to Sweden.

I must confess you one thing, and I think you understand me as you have yourself children. It hasn't been an easy time for me to wait my third child, who was born in December 1945. To be homeless, to be never quite secure not to be sent back to Russia – that is just as a stone on my heart.

But Lübeck was a time of hope in many ways. Meta was able to busy herself with the children, trying to establish a little order and placidity at last. Henno often played cards with other Estonians and they gathered wood for the cooking fires, while Meta sewed long trousers for Ann and Mai and made warm linings for their coats. She had only one dress throughout her pregnancy with Jaan, and many times she washed it in the evening, hoping it would be dry enough to put on the next day.

Perhaps I take things too seriously. I know Jaan is a dear little boy; he is growing older and it isn't so difficult any more to deal with him – but there is one "but"...

What was the one "but"? She had written earlier, when Ann was born, that she didn't want a boy yet. Was it that she saw boys as potential soldiers?

Henno is very proud of his son...

I loved the photos of Mai, Ann and Jaan that she sent. In one, they sat astride a bench in a row of descending heights. Jaan, in front, had the shortest of short trousers I'd ever seen, and wide braces which I found utterly bewitching. Mum talked about them all very readily and must have told me a little about their journeyings. In my mind their escape from Estonia was interwoven with Joseph and Mary's flight into Egypt with baby Jesus; as far as I was concerned Meta was taken on a donkey to Pärnu. I've just noticed that they lived for a while in *a carpenter's workroom with stone floor.* This must have added to my confusion.

Mum was far too protective to tell told me anything alarming, but I must have caught something of her emotions as she repeated the story and added to it. I began to have nightmares. In my dream I was surrounded by soft, white, billowing stuff rather like cotton wool. As long as it stayed in this sort of cumulus state, all was well; but sometimes lumps would begin to thin and tease apart like wool ready for spinning. When this happened I was frightened, and if the lumps grew thinner and thinner then pulled and snapped, I woke screaming. At least, I wanted to scream but, terrifyingly, no sound would come. I can still conjure up that helpless feeling of voicelessness. At last the screams would emerge and Mum or Dad would be by my side. I could never explain what was wrong, but those dreams are still with me.

Peacetime

In May 1946 we came to Sweden. How quietly and simply Meta announces their arrival. It was all she ever said to Mum about it.

At first they were quarantined on one of the beautiful islands of the archipelago and Ann, just over three years old by now, would dimly remember it as a lovely place. Henno had gone ahead of them and found temporary work in a hospital, and Meta had to cope alone with the two little girls and baby Jaan. She was disconcerted by the indignity of being made to strip for the medical inspection by male and female doctors; she felt like a criminal rather than a refugee. Mai was deeply distressed by the process and refused to let anyone but Meta undress her. Ann was helped by a nurse and remembered ever after her resentment that Mai, her *older* sister, had Mummy to look after her while she, the *younger* one, had to be good and let a strange woman take off her clothes. Jaan wasn't old enough to mind.

As a child absorbing what Mum told me from Meta's letters, I found the reality of Meta's life was both horrifying and exciting. I fantasised about my new 'cousins' while Mum tried to be practical. She wanted to transport Meta and Henno and the children to England and, to that end, tried to find out whether Henno could work as a doctor here. At last her guilt could be channelled into practical action. Meta was delighted with the idea, but cautious too:

19.3.47

To come to England – that has been Henno's dream for a long time. Is there any possibility? I am afraid Henno can't work there as a physician

*and what else can he do there? And I haven't been working for years.
I have best memories from my stay in England. Your parents and you
have been very kind to me. I was so happy to live in a real English
family instead of a hostel.*

*You have twice asked me whether Henno knows any English or
not. In Lübeck a year ago Henno knew English quite well. He was
reading English books and he had much practice with Mil-Gar. and
UNRRA officers, while [because] he was the camp doctor and besides
working in Estonian Red Cross. Now, of course, he has forgotten a
little, for he has studied Swedish. He can speak Swedish quite well. It
is a pity – I cannot, for I have really no time and no possibility. I can
speak only as much as that is needed to do my shoppings. I am between
these four walls and get very little out of doors. I don't see any other
Estonians and I feel myself very alone. In Stocksund are living very
few [of] our country people.*

*Thankyou for your kind asking if I need anything – but I don't
need really anything. Sweden is a rich, rich country and here you can
buy what you wish – only you must have a lot of money.*

Meta went to look in the shops in Stockholm on her own for the first
time and found herself gazing at fur coats. She laughed at her stupidity – and
would do so again many years later – for being transfixed by something so
extravagant, rather than feasting her eyes on the many small necessities she'd
been without for so long.

*There is shortage of no things. The Swedish people don't understand
what is war – they haven't had war for two hundred years. They
have had peace. They have had money and they have had their
homes and relatives and friends. But they have been kind to us – to
all refugees, they let us work and earn money and have our daily
bread. And when I have just enough plain food for my children
and a lodging and enough clothes – that will do. I am really
thankful to you – but I am getting on with that what I have. And
in summer Henno will be earning more money. Only then we must
be separated. Henno will be in different towns in Sweden, I am
staying here. I wish we could find a flat for our family, but there is
just shortage of flats.*

That is a pity that your parents are working as hard as that. When [if] your mother has no time to write to me, I understand her very well. You will write me all the news and I am contented with that. Please give my best greetings to your mother and father and your sister and her husband. Does Mrs Parkinson (snr) remember me? Will you, please greet her.

Best wishes to you and your husband and children
Yours loving friend
Meta

P.S. Will you please excuse my handwriting. I have been writing this letter many days. I am just never quite alone and I am never quite free and there is very little time left for myself. I wish a good Easter-time to all.

So many things in this letter struck a chord with you, didn't they, Mum? You knew what it was like to feel lonely and isolated from your own people. The anguish of being parted from your husband was something which you never came to terms with. How paltry your sorrows seemed beside Meta's fearful experiences – the separations from Henno when there was no certainty of ever seeing him again. Even Henno's search for a job mocked and diminished your own anxieties, since Dad knew throughout the war that his job was there waiting for him. The one thing that you could really latch on to – did it perhaps represent a sort of expiation? – was the search for a home. You still so relished your own house and wanted Meta to share the security of a family home – a little peacetime corner of Estonia in the vast, strange land of Sweden – or, better still, a place in England, where Meta had once been so happy.

Nan too was willing to move heaven and earth to bring Meta and her family to England, and wrote with typical generosity:

20.4.47

Meta My Dear,

Phyll showed me your last letter to her and I feel very sad to know what you have suffered. I see you say it is in your dream to come to England. Meta, if you <u>do</u> Father Shaw and myself will give you *a loving and hearty welcome for you to come and stay with us until you could get a flat or house.*

I believe your husband could practise his profession here as there is a house near us full of German refugees and one of the husbands is a doctor. He works at a local mental hospital. I'll make some enquiries if I can get to know where to enquire.

We have two rooms which you could use and of course the kitchen and scullery to cook and eat in. We would be so happy for you to be here and you would have no rent to pay you know dear and the children would be loved and welcomed so much, bless you all you poor dears.

Well Meta dear with kind greetings to your husband and a kiss to all three bairns and a heap of love to your dear self.

Your affectionate friend,

E. Shaw

But all of both Mum's and Nan's good efforts came to nothing:

1.6.47

My Dear Meta,

[...] I have been trying to get permission for you all to come to England, when I received the letter which I enclose. I was so very disappointed, I knew you would be disappointed too, and I have waited for courage to be able to tell you this news. But even now I am not giving up hope and am writing to other people about it. In case you do not know, the B.M.A. is the British Medical Association.

I am wondering how long it will take to save up enough money for me to come and visit you! The cost of living is very high here just now. Everything costs quite 2 times as much as when you were here in 1938 and some things are 3 or more times as expensive. But we are very happy in our little house with our own little garden. Our children are a great joy to us and we feel that even if we have to go without a lot of things we would like, yet we have the things that mean most in life.

I wonder how much news you ever have in the Swedish papers about life in Britain. So many people abroad seem to think that we are starving. That is certainly not so. We have quite enough food and

I believe that the nation's standard of health is higher now than before the war. There is not so much variety in our diet as pre-war and I for one do miss all the fruit we used to import, but some day things will improve and under our rationing scheme we all have a fair share of food.

In our little garden we are growing a few vegetables – lettuces, beans and beetroot etc. but we have not room to grow much. My mother has hens in her garden now so we have a good supply of eggs.

All our children under 5 yrs are allowed 1 pint of milk each day at 2d a pint and for very poor people this is free of charge. Extra eggs and cod liver oil and orange juice are allowed on each ration book of all children up to 5 yrs. These things cost very little as there is a government subsidy [...]

Perhaps you are having lovely summer sunshine as we are now. Do you remember how hot and lovely the weather was most of the time when I came to stay with you in your beloved Eesti? It is like that here now and we are all loving it.

Oh my dear, how I wish we could do something to repay you and Henno for many of the things you have suffered.

Greetings of course to Henno and so much to your dear self,
Phyllis

It had taken Mum several weeks to pluck up the courage to write this letter, with its disappointing news. She waited guiltily for Meta's reply, wishing so much that she hadn't raised Meta's hopes before checking the possibilities. Four weeks later Meta wrote:

30.6.47
Stocksund, Sweden

My dear, dear Phyllis,
I received your letter a long time ago. I was not disappointed – no, not at all, because 1 know that all before. That is all clear to us, but we still have our thoughts and dreams after all. Henno does know it that he cannot work as a physician in England. He thinks perhaps there is just some other work he can do, that is somehow connected with his study and knowledge. Of course it would be easier for us now

to come to England, than if we would be in Lübeck (Germany). But our fate has brought us to Sweden. I should have answered you at once, that you needn't worry as much as that – it comes like it must come. Many, many thanks that you think of us so much.

Last three weeks have been very worrying for me. On 10th June Henno went to Borås (a town in South Sweden) for the whole summer. He can work there as a doctor and he is earning there quite enough money to be content. After Henno's departure I fell ill – I had a temperature and terrible headache and my throat was sore. But as there wasn't any other people to help me, I could not be in bed. Some days later Mai and Jaan fell ill at the same time. Mai recovered after three days, then Ann had to lie some days in bed. Jaan had high temperature but his ear was festering and he couldn't go out. The weather is hot and there is much sunshine. And to be in a room – just under the roof – oh – it was a pain for Jaan and me. Today we visit the doctor. Now Jaan can go out, but we must be careful. It was very hard for me that Henno wasn't at home. It makes me so tired when the children are ill. I am this summer for the first time in my life in a town and I feel myself like in prison. I know – all will pass – this summer as well as others. But I feel sometimes that I have some little wishes and I don't want to be so alone and homeless.

Your idea to come and visit us is just delightful. Oh – it would be nice to have you here. I wish I could have a flat for my family where I could receive you. I hope this dream will be fulfilled.

Sadly this visit never happened, as there was no money for such a trip.

For the next few months Mum was mortified by her lack of success in waving a magic wand to transport Meta to England, and somehow couldn't bring herself to write. There seemed so little to say, except things that would highlight her own increasing happiness and security in contrast to Meta's situation. Eventually Meta couldn't wait any longer, and wrote again:

5.9.47
Stocksund, Sweden

My dearest Phyllis,
I have been waiting for your letter a long time. How are you

getting on and how has been your summer? Did your husband get a long holiday? Did you go to the sea-side? We have had here a very warm summer and there has been but few rainy days. It has been too little rain and the soil is dry and grass looks like burned.

I am sorry I troubled you and your dear mother so much with our idea to come to England. We are getting on now much better here in Sweden. Henno had a work as a doctor the whole summer in a town hospital in Borås. There is much hope that he will get a regular work in Borås for a long time from the beginning of November. When we can find a flat in Borås we can go there as well.

Henno is delighted of that idea to go to live in West Sweden, for the moment at any rate! We do not know how long will Russia be as far as that and then it is better to have the open sea to take a voyage to some other free country. [Presumably she means 'should the need arise to flee again'.]

I promised you in my last letter in June to write to you more about my children and their interests. Mai – eldest daughter – doesn't yet go to school. In Sweden the children start learning when they are seven – usually. In last winter Mai and Ann didn't go to the kindergarten, but they will do that this winter when we are settled in Borås. There are no other Estonian children in the neighbourhood and the girls have to play with Swedish children and so they learn by and by the Swedish language. Mai and Ann are great friends and they play much together. Mai is much livelier and she doesn't take the life and things too serious. She is a little bit nervous child – perhaps she has seen and remembers too much things we have seen during our journeys. She likes to talk. Ann is more quiet and [...] she knows how to require what are her rights. Ann seems to have more time to think and ask. Ann is more fond of dolls than Mai. Little Jaan is very troublesome for the girls. He disturbs very much their play and wants the same toys as the girls. Jaan learns to talk and he is very interesting with his plays and imitations.

I do wait that we can get a flat in Borås. I don't want to live and work another winter in such a close room and so many people together. It is so very, very tiresome.

I wish you all the best. Many greetings from Henno to you and

your husband and the same from me. I wish you could write to me as
soon as possible!
   Yours affectionate,
   Meta

Meta may have been disappointed that she had to wait a couple of weeks for the reply.

28.9.47

My dear Meta,
   How I hope with all my heart that you will find just the flat that you need in Borås and be together and never separated any more. I can imagine how delighted Ann and Mai will be if you have a flat. I remember so well when we came to this little house just over a year ago, how very happy Peter was that at last we had our very own home all together – Daddy, Mummy, Peter and Hazel. It was something we had not known before and we are very, very thankful, for there are still many young married people without a home, but just living with their parents.
   We have a little garden too, and the children have wonderful games there. We have several old wooden packing cases and planks of wood. These become engines, ships, motor cars and many other things according to the game they are playing! What a joy it is to observe them at play.

Those wooden packing cases and planks suddenly evoke such memories. We had our very own home-made see-saw, which wobbled rather alarmingly. I can feel the rough grain under my hands as I gripped the plank and waited for the alternate lurch and bump of tummy and bottom. There is a photo of me at the height of the upward swoop, mouth slightly open in ecstasy.

30.11.47
Stocksund, Sweden

My dear Phyllis,
   I have your letter and photographs already a long, long time.

Many thanks! Days have passed so quickly, I have always so much to do. And all the time I have been waiting to tell you that I have a flat – a home. I haven't it yet but I hope to get it in a fortnight. I am alone again. Henno has got work in Borås in the same hospital, where he was working last summer, from 15th November. He is working at his profession and he is very happy. That is something to have regular work and to earn money. Doctor's salary is quite a good one. Therefore we could just send you and your family a small parcel for Christmas. I know that these provisions I put in are all rationed in your country. These provisions are unrationed in this country. And to have all rationed, I know what it means. I hope that you and your family will enjoy these things.

I am really waiting very much to get my own flat and kitchen – more place for children to play and work. It is just too close and the children are nervous as well, when they can't be alone and undisturbed for a while. When I read your letter about your children and their plays, I understood how much my children have lost not having their own home and a regular life. And I myself have lost much of my energy and good will and it seems to me sometimes that I have forgotten all that I have read about education.

Life has often been only waiting that days should pass quicker. And we refugees sometimes think that we are just vegetating. That was and is still [in] Germany. Here in Sweden – we can all find work and that makes a great difference. Could you understand me? I don't want to complain (lament), but to tell you how very different I feel and act.

Now I ask one thing from you? Could you send me a book about education? Just an easy one, everyday simple questions. I must brush up my memory and try to think more and a book will help me. Please don't smile! I hope to have more time to read in my new home in future. Oh, dear Phyllis, I just wish to talk with you about so many problems.

Books and reading were as important in my parents' home as in Meta's, and Phyll had taken several to Estonia with her in 1939. Meta's books had, of course, all been destroyed, and in any case were impossible to carry when she fled.

I do hope that I can go to Borås before Christmas.

Many, many greetings to you and your family and with best wishes and much love to you from
Meta

Mum felt intensely humbled by Meta's letter and so wished she could be of more help and emotional support to her. The promised Christmas parcel arrived:

8.1.48

My dear Meta,

What a grand parcel you so kindly sent us this Christmas time! Thank you very, very much. The things are all most welcome and being greatly enjoyed by us all. The children were especially delighted to see so much chocolate. It is so very dear of you to think of us and send us such a splendid parcel – you, who have lost so very, very much and yet can give so generously to us. It makes me feel that I shall weep, my dear, dear friend. Thank you so much [...]

That wonderful Christmas parcel is something I thought I'd made up. It seems so unlikely for a refugee to send us a food parcel – but there it is. I do remember the chocolate, and could there have been butter? I am quite sure that Mum wept, as she would do on many subsequent occasions when parcels arrived from Meta, containing many different things over the years. I can still hear her special way of saying, "It's from Meta."

And now I have to apologise because I have not written to thank you sooner. Just before Christmas when the parcel arrived, both the children were very poorly. They had bad coughs and colds and though Peter soon got better, Hazel had to be kept in bed and had to have a fire burning day and night. (Oh how I long for central heating!) Then I too caught the germ and was very unwell myself. I think I felt worse because I have another baby coming. It is just the beginning of the third month now and I am feeling much better. But it has all meant that I have only been able to look after the children and cook the meals. I have felt very guilty and unkind and

do hope you will forgive me, my dear. I have thought of you and your
kindness so often.

She thought too of how it must have been for Meta – pregnant with
Jaan, living in a camp and with only one dress – and her guilt weighed even
heavier.

[...] You poor darling! How well I understand when you say you feel
you have forgotten all you know about education. You have had to go
through so many horrors and face so many difficulties.
[...] May this New Year bring much joy and gladness to you and
Henno.
Much love to you. I will write again soon.
Phyllis

She did indeed write soon, and sent a parcel for Meta.

15.2.48
Borås, Sweden

My dear, dear Phyllis,
My best thanks to you for your letter and your books. That is really
too much from you to send me your own book. I am glad to have these
two books. I found a list of my translations between the pages of your
book and there came so many good old memories from that time I was
living in your house. I hope you don't miss your book very much, and
perhaps you can replace it very soon. If not, I shall send you back your
book after I have studied it for a while.

While working at the Methodist Mission House before the war, Mum had
been encouraged by Mu – now, of course, her sister-in-law – to take a Sunday
School class, and had derived much enjoyment in the challenge of teaching
small children, albeit for a short while once a week. It sparked such an interest
that she bought an instructional book for infant teachers, and it must have
been this that she sent to Meta. At the time, books were relatively expensive,
and sending her own copy was not merely an act of generosity on Mum's
part. She could only afford to buy one new book in addition, since money

was very tight. In this way, she was able to send two books to Meta. The irony never escaped Mum that Meta's refugee family continued to be so much better off than her secure one – a disparity in wealth that increased as the years progressed.

The letter continued:

I am so glad you wrote me about yourself. I think you are very happy. I hope you feel yourself better now. How are the children? Is Peter well now and did Hazel catch chicken pox? It is the worst thing to have the children unwell at home.

My children haven't had anything serious up to now. I am so glad this winter for I have a warm flat. I have central heating and I have a very equal warmth in every room during day and night. The children are very lightly dressed and I do not freeze myself. I am pleased to have this small comfortable flat in a new built house. I feel myself quite another people – although I feel myself very often terribly tired. The children feel themselves much better too. They have now place for their toys and games and they have place to run about. It seems to me that little Jaan is developing now quickly. He has learnt many words and he is chattering all day long. Especially during that time when Mai and Ann are in the kindergarten. It is a private kindergarten and the girls go there only three hours a day. It is a Swedish kindergarten and I am sorry for that. But the children must learn Swedish properly, for they have to go to Swedish schools – Mai already next autumn. I myself am not able to speak Swedish and am getting on very slowly.

As Ann much later told me, both Meta and Henno really hoped to return to Estonia one day. There was quite a community of Estonians who had found refuge in Sweden, although Meta didn't mention any she had met in Borås. Despite living in Sweden, Mai, Ann and Jaan were brought up as Estonian children, and this wasn't always easy for them. At seventeen Ann assured me seriously that she could never marry a Swedish boy – then not many years later she did just that.

15.4.48
Borås, Sweden

My dearest Phyllis,

Thankyou for the lovely Easter card. I am wondering how you are. I haven't had a letter from you for a long time. I sent you a letter in February. Have you got it? I understand you so well – I know you have so much to do and I know that all isn't now as easy and fluent to you as it would be otherwise. I hope that you are well and that your husband and children are well.

We have now for a while a regular life, and the days are passing ever so quickly when you have good days and peace and harmony. My husband has his work and is busy all the day long. He is going at 8 o'clock in the morning and returning home at 7 o'clock in the evening, sometimes even later. He has night watch every other night and is free every other Sunday.

It sounds a punishing schedule, with night duty on alternate nights and the only time they could be sure of being together as a family was on every other Sunday. Yet Meta could happily speak of harmony, peace and good days.

Mai and Ann are going to the kindergarten five times in a week and they do it with pleasure. The girls have learnt a lot of Swedish and they pronounce Swedish quite properly. Little Jaan is learning to speak Estonian and he is a friendly and jolly boy.

For a while we Estonian refugees felt that we aren't very safe here in Sweden, and many of us are thinking how to go away from Sweden and to get to America. Of course they have right – to be as far away as possible from Russia, but we haven't yet any reason to panic. Our family hasn't made any preparations for leaving Sweden already. Naturally we have our suspicions, and we don't know what may happen, and it isn't impossible that one day we are travellers again.

On April 6th 1948 the YYA treaty was signed between Finland and Russia, whereby Finland was obliged to deter any possible attacks by Allied Powers, either on Finland or on Russia via Finland. Finland could theoretically request the aid of Russian troops in the event of an attack on its territory. By this means the Soviet Union could influence Finland's internal political affairs, although it *apparently* recognised Finland's autonomy and wish to remain neutral in the Cold War. This was an anxiety for Estonian refugees in Sweden, since any reneging on the pact on the side of the Russians created the possibility of Russian troops in Finland, which was altogether too close for comfort. It was thus for a time seen as a real threat – hence the idea of flight to America.

4.5.48

My dear Meta,

I am very guilty for the long delay in writing to you. I think though that my last letter must have been lost on the way, because I know you should have had a letter from me not very long ago.

I think of you so often and wish that I could see your three children. How very much we have been thinking of you as we have read of the pact the Finns have made with Russia. The troubles of the world are far from over, but we hope with all our hearts that another and more ghastly war will not come. It is not easy for us here to have faith in the future – yet we are settled in our own house in our own country. How very much harder it is for you who have had to leave your own home and country. My heart aches for you and I wish so much that I could do something to help you. I hope and hope that you do not have to leave Sweden and start travelling on again. It makes me sad to think you may have to go as far as America some day, for then I feel I might never see you again for I don't think that for many years I could save enough money to travel to America.

However, in spite of all that is so sad in the world today, we have to keep joyous and happy for the sake of our children. Their lives are so unspoiled by the ugly things of life.

I was interested to read about your three children and glad that Mai and Ann are happy to go to kindergarten. Peter loves his school and seems to take an interest in everything. Hazel wants to go to school but they cannot take her yet for they have so many pupils. Because of the war there is a shortage of teachers and many of the schools are overcrowded.

Both Hazel and Peter are greatly looking forward to the coming of our baby and ask so many questions about it. It is so lovely to feel that they can share with George and me in this way. Hazel plays a lot with her dolls like a little mother.

I will write again very soon. Much love to you and the children and my greetings to Henno. He must be very glad to be able to follow his own profession again.
  Your loving
  Phyllis

For once, it was Meta who proved slow to respond:

15.7.48
Borås, Sweden

My dear, dear Phyllis,
  I have been really very naughty not having written to you for so long time. Excuse me, but I do not know how the days are passing ever so quickly and I always have something to do. But I have been thinking of you very, very often and wonder if it is time to congratulate you. I think you have passed a very hard time – I felt myself always tired in the last months. And having the whole housekeeping without any help – there is much to do and it is all tiresome with small children.
  We are getting on quite well. Meantime it seemed to be quite quiet in the big wide world, but now it is much talked about the possibilities of the coming war. It is clear that nobody wants another war, but on the other hand there is a question – how will it be all right and clear without a war? We don't believe that Mr Stalin will ever give up the Baltic States, Poland and all the other countries without any fighting. No – never!

Anxieties about a further war may well have been triggered by the Soviet blockade of Berlin. Contrary to the Russian demand for a totally disarmed Germany, the Americans felt that only a rearmed Germany could provide a defence against any threat of Russia's future expansion into Western Europe. Berlin was divided into four zones, controlled by Russia in the East and the Allies to the West. In May 1946, America had stopped shipments of goods to the Russian zone, part of an earlier agreement, and by December the British and American zones combined, and were joined by the French zone some months later. By June 1948 negotiations between the Russians and Americans had completely broken down, and on June 24th Soviet forces blocked rail and road lines into West Berlin. All goods, including coal, had to be airlifted into West Berlin, which, fortunately, was unhampered by Russian air strikes.

We wish very much that we could stay here in Sweden as long as there is a need to stay away from home. We have no mind to go to America, for there we have to start once again and Henno cannot work there in his profession. Here we have made the first steps and we have our little home and we have here our Estonian and Swedish friends. The country and its inhabitants are now a little familiar to us. But we don't wish to stay here for ever – we should like to go back to our native country, though there will be many difficulties to surpass.

In last time I have been thinking very much of my parents and brother. Sometimes I am going to lose my hope to see them again, for there has passed many years since I saw them last. And they are living in very bad circumstances, especially my father, who has been now seven years in Siberia. And there is little hope to see my brother again, for as much as we have heard most of Estonian young men were deported to east Russia, where they are working in the most miserable conditions. Perhaps is my mother still living – although she wasn't very well when I last saw her. But I must keep hoping and I am often talking with Ann and Mai about their native country. Mai is remembering little from my mother's home, Ann doesn't know anything. It is difficult to keep the few memories for the children and after some years my children are more Swedish than Estonian. Mai is going to a Swedish school next month and this is not easy for me.

We are staying in town the whole summer. Henno has no holidays and so I don't want to go away with the children and leave Henno alone. We have been separated too much and it is nice to have the whole family together for a longer time. During Whitsuntide Henno's sister visited us for three days. Peep was staying with Henno's mother in Stocksund. In August Henno's mother is having her holidays and she will come to stay with us. She is longing for Ann, Mai and Jaan, especially for Jaan. Jaan is a jolly little boy, very lively and impulsive. I think he is now in his most interesting age for us.

It would of course be very lovely to go to the seaside or to a country place for some weeks, but we hope to do this next summer.

The children

The weather has been since the middle of May rather cold with little sunshine. It is often raining and the children must be indoors. Therefore we don't wish very much to go away from town. And we have roads [footpaths?] *and land just near our house and can take walks and gather leaves and berries.*

When is George having his holidays? [I note that this is the first time she has mentioned him by name, always referring to him as 'your husband'.] *Are you going away from town?* [She has obviously forgotten how heavily pregnant Phyllis is by this time, making the idea of a holiday somewhat unrealistic.] *I wish you a bright holiday weather! I wish you all the best for summer and all the coming days.*

I am sending you a photo from my children – they look like this now. [Is this the one I remember so well with the three children arranged in size order sitting astride a bench, Jaan in front sporting the wonderful braces?]

17.10.48

My dear Meta,

I think you must be wondering what has happened to me and I am a very naughty person not to have written to you sooner than this. I received you last letter together with the lovely photo of your children exactly 3 months ago. Did Henno take the photo? It really is delightful and you must be very proud to have such lovely children. I think Ann looks more like you than the other two. Is that so?

I am wondering of [if] you would like me to send you copies of some of the photographs I took in that summer long ago when we were so happy and I stayed with you in your charming country. I think perhaps you have no pictures to show your children of their native country? Shall I do this? Oh my dear! How my heart aches for you so far away from your own country and knowing little or nothing of what has happened to your own family. I am so ashamed that I ever get dispirited or discontented.

Perhaps because she didn't want to depress Meta, Phyllis never mentioned that George's younger brother was now married to an Austrian–Jewish refugee who also had no knowledge as yet of the fate of her parents. They lived close to us and Mum couldn't have failed to be aware of her sister-in-law's anguish.

And now I must tell you our special news and that is that we had a baby daughter on August 2nd. She was born during the afternoon and did not take long to come and I soon felt well and strong again. She is a dear little baby, strong and happy, already smiling and making those lovely little sounds that are so entertaining to a mother's ear. We call her Rosemary and she is greatly loved by us all. Hazel and Peter are very pleased to welcome her into our family and like to help me at bath times. It is so satisfying to have a tiny baby to look after again. I now have someone to help me in the house two mornings each week, but I find life very busy. [Much later I realised this help was generously paid for by one of my aunts, as were many of the Guernsey holidays we enjoyed] *However, I keep very well and am so happy and content. There are times when I wonder just how right it is to bring children into the world – I feel that in a way we are failing them. They are so happy and innocent of the storms that are gathering again over mankind. And yet there is so little that one can do to influence public opinion and sway the balance against war and devastation.*

We too did not go on holiday this year. Rosemary was born just a week after the school holidays began and we could not therefore go away together. However, Peter and Hazel went to stay with my sister, Twink, and Alan in the country village of Frodsham. They greatly enjoyed themselves. It is a much freer life for children in the country than in the town.

My memories of this time are not nearly as glowing and happy as Mum's. But Pete and I were indeed tickled pink when we were told that a new baby was on the way. It must have been a fairly solemn announcement as we were in the sitting room, the seldom used, little front room. There wasn't much furniture but we'd recently had a new, very cheap and very hairy pale green carpet put down. For some reason Pete and I were left alone for a few minutes, and we talked about how funny it would be to have an extra person in the family. Our excitement became positively hysterical and we rolled around on the floor in fits of giggles. Our pleasure was short-lived when Mum came back and found us covered in wiry carpet pile which stuck to our clothes and wouldn't brush out. She was furious. No doubt she later went away and felt guilty about spoiling the moment – but we didn't know that.

I enjoyed the preparations for the baby, and helped stack nappies, clothes and bedding. My dolls had practice runs in the wicker baby cradle. But shortly before Rosa was due, I developed measles and was very poorly. It must have been an awful problem for Mum. They didn't want to endanger the baby – so I was sent away to be ill at 88, Grandma and Grandpa's house in Croydon. It took me a long time to forgive them for this, and it didn't do a lot for my future relationship with my baby sister. Kind Auntie Mu and Grandma nursed me and read to me endlessly in a darkened room, and there was medicine on a sugar lump – what a treat! But they were not my mother – *she* was putting the finishing touches to my baby sister, and I felt unloved and jealous that this baby, who wasn't even born yet, had made me go away. There wasn't a telephone, so I couldn't even speak to Mum, although Dad visited me from his office just down the road.

Once I was well enough I played in the garden. It was a big garden, with plenty of variety for a child to enjoy. There were areas of grass and flowers, a forest of raspberry canes you could crawl into and a wonderful mulberry tree which spewed juicy, fat berries onto the grass where they stained hands, knees and clothes most gloriously. I was hiding in the raspberry canes when Auntie Mu came to tell me I had a baby sister. She was surprised at my indifference. Later I cried. They thought I wanted to see the baby, but really I was mourning the loss of my toy rabbit's eyes. It was a peculiar bunny, with a blue plush head and floral cotton body like a tea cosy, but I loved him. He had glass eyes on metal stalks, and I'd discovered that they could be pulled out on those stalks in a grotesque and satisfying way that Pete would have relished. Somehow or other I'd overdone the pulling without realising it, and the glass eyes were lost among the raspberry canes. Grandma kindly replaced them with buttons – far safer – but I never felt the same about him again. In some vague way it all seemed to be my sister's fault.

I went home for a few days when Rosa – she was rarely called 'Rosemary' – was about a week old, and the sight of a real, live baby in the wicker basket reconciled me to her briefly. Then I was sent off again – this time, thankfully, with Pete. We were put on a train to Chester, labels tied to our coat buttons, and met at the other end by Uncle Alan. I suppose Mum and Dad felt we would benefit from a holiday with our cousins in the country, but it also freed them to enjoy the baby without us, and I resented this madly for years.

However, by the time Mum was writing this letter I was very much in line for being centre stage again, thanks to my recurring sore throats.

Next week I have to take Hazel to a throat specialist to have his advice about her tonsils. Ever since she had whooping cough (pertussis) two years ago one of her tonsils has been frequently inflamed and if she

*has a cold, she also develops a severe cough. At present she is very well
and a course of sunlight treatment is proving of great benefit to her.*

Oh, those coughs! In my memory I spent much of my early childhood
nights coughing. It was better if I didn't lie flat on my back, so Mum and
Dad would lay a chair on its side on the bed; it was a cane-seated one which
made enchanting patterns on your skin if you sat bare-bottomed on it. To
this chair they strapped a pillow and me. Inevitably, during the night my
moorings came loose and I woke, barking like a sea lion before I was quietened
and tethered again. I smell still the oil fire burning and see the flower petal
pattern of its top reflected on the ceiling.

*P.S. Hazel has drawn the enclosed "letter" for you all – quite her own
idea. She specially wished me to send amongst the photos the one of her
on a see-saw in the garden.*

    *The weather is becoming colder and we are having a good deal
of rain now. How I wish we had central heating! If ever we are able
to have a house built specially for us, I shall have no fireplaces, but
central heating and radiators and hot pipes!* [Sadly, she had to wait
years for this.]

    *[...] Yesterday the throat specialist saw Hazel and said she will
have to have her tonsils removed. They are infected and have pus in
them. Henno will know all about this operation. It may not be for
several months as there are many children waiting.*

    *I suppose Peep is a big boy now. He was just a tiny fellow when
I saw him. I hope your sister-in-law and Mrs Lender are well. Please
give them my greetings when you write to them. They too have suffered
much because of the war and I am sad for them.*

    Again my love to you my dear, dear Meta.
    Phyllis

26.11.48
Borås

Dear Phyllis,
    Many, many thanks for your letter and photos you have sent me.

Especially many thanks to Hazel for her nice photo on the see-saw and as well for her letter and drawings. I am so glad you are all well. I am so glad for all has gone so well with you dear Phyllis. I am looking often at your photos and I think you have lovely children and you have much joy of them. Does Hazel look more like you? And Peter has such an enterprising face. I suppose he has always his head full of good ideas! I am glad you have another daughter. I have always missed a sister and now I am glad to have two daughters and you have the same. I think it must be lovely to have a sister. You have of course much work with your children and especially with the baby – but you have also much entertainment.

Now I am going to tell you our news. Henno was two months – September, October – without work and now he is in a hospital in Gällivare in Lapland since the end of October. Gällivare is a small town in the very North of Sweden and Henno is quite a long way far from us. Henno is having there very cold weather and much snow and very little daylight at all. Henno is going to stay in Gällivare two-three months and he is not coming home for Christmas, because it is a very long way to come to us and go back (one way over 30 hours). And besides he can't come away and leave his work. Of course I am not very delighted we are separated again, but Henno has to work and to earn money and there wasn't any other vacant place somehow nearer. And Henno wouldn't be a long time there. Perhaps Henno's mother is coming to visit us during Xmas. It isn't very sure because my mother-in-law doesn't feel herself quite well. She has had heavy rheumatic pains a fortnight ago and wants to rest. It is also a long journey from Stockholm to us (8 hours) and during Xmas the trains are rather full. Our children are very much waiting for Xmas – I suppose all children do wait Xmas and wish to have many nice things.

Mai is very fond of school and she is interested in all that she has to do in school. She can pronounce Swedish correctly like a Swedish child, but she doesn't master the language. But she learns every day new words. At home Mai is playing with Ann and Jaan and Jaan is understanding the play as well as the girls.

It is really kind of you if you can send me some copies of these photographs you took in that summer long ago when we were so happy

*and you stayed with us in our dear country. I haven't got any of these
with me and it would be interesting to show these to my children and
I should like to see them myself.*

*How is Hazel feeling herself? When is she going to have her tonsils
removed? I think it isn't very dangerous and the children have it much
easier than the grown-ups.*

*Did I tell you Ann had an operation last spring? Her nose tonsil
or third tonsil (I don't know how you name it)* [adenoids?] *was
operated. Before the operation she could not breathe correctly when
she was sleeping and she often had bad dreams and was waking at
night crying. After the operation she is all right now. She is sleeping
well and has no bad dreams. All our children have now sunlight
treatment. I have got a lamp at home and that makes it easier for
me than to go to the hospital to have it there. My children like it very
much to have sunlight when there is no sunlight outside.*

I remember this treatment very well and can still conjure up the smell of
the clinic where I had to go. There was a thick hessian carpet on the floor and
on the stairs, so coarse that there was potential to graze a knee if you tripped.
On the landing at the top was a wonderful rocking horse with dappled
sides, flowing mane and glorious leather bridle with bells, but we were never
allowed to ride it. I imagine the squabbles over taking turns were more than
the nurses wished to cope with. We undressed and donned goggles or a rather
handsome visor before being led into a room with a warm blue lamp. What
followed was boring in the extreme as there was nothing to do but sit, and
as the other children were all strangers we didn't even talk. It was a popular
therapy at the time and died out, on the whole, with the development of
antibiotics. There were also, apparently, increasing fears of skin cancer as the
relationship between sun exposure and carcinoma became apparent. I was
interested to discover that it was popular in Sweden too.

*Did Peter receive my letter with the postage stamps? Could he use
these? Has he any special wishes? Is he interested to get more later
when Henno is coming back from Borås?*

*Sometimes I have a great wish to see you and your family, and
I suppose, we should have much to tell each other. Only when is
coming that day!*

After that first flush of writing there are longer gaps between letters, with apologies on both sides. Both women are aware of all the so many things they could say face to face, but have to content themselves with exchanging news of the children and of the essentially trivial happenings in their lives. They are no longer bubbly young women with the world at their feet, but adults who had experienced emotions they could not have dreamt of a few years before. But, however changed their circumstances, the warm core of their friendship endured – or, in Meta's words, *I am richer now to have you again.*

Post-war dream?

27.7.49
Borås, Sweden

My dear, dear Phyllis,

*   It is really a very very long time past since we last wrote to each other. I am afraid that some of our letters have got lost on the way. I have been waiting for a letter from you for a very long time. Many times I have begun to write to you but I have not finished those. I am interested how you have spent your winter and what you are doing in the summer? How are the children getting on at school? Does Hazel like to go to school? Does she want to do all the interesting things she has to do at school? How is Rosemary getting on? Is she beginning to walk now? Rosemary is going to have her birthday very soon now. Many happy returns to her on this day.*

How badly Mum felt for neglecting Meta, but she found it hard looking after three children with very little money, and was often depressed. This made her feel even more guilty as, compared to Meta, she felt that she had so little to complain about. She had a husband who came home every day, while Meta saw Henno only every so often. Her home was in England, her own country, not in an alien one with so many terrible memories of flight and fear. Meta never held this against her.

Our days are passing quickly enough. On June we had very bad weather

– it was raining and cold. On July it has been a brilliant weather with much sunshine. In the beginning of June Mai finished her first school year. Ann can't go to school next year for she is too young, although she wants to go very much.

As in many European countries, the age for starting school was two years later than in England.

Last winter I have been very much alone with the children in Borås. Henno has had to work in different towns in Sweden for shorter and longer periods. Henno was staying with us the whole of June. Now he is working in the hospital in Stocksund for two months. (We were living in Stocksund two years ago). Mai and Ann are now in an Estonian children's summerhouse (I suppose you know what I mean, I don't know the right name) for one month (17.07 – 11.08). [Presumably a summer camp.] *The girls are very pleased to be among the other Estonian children and they are spending there very jolly days. Next week I am going to take Jaan on a journey to Stocksund for a fortnight. I am going to stay at my mother-in-law's home and I can meet Henno, for the hospital is very close to my mother-in-law's home. My mother-in-law is waiting for us very much. We haven't seen her for a long time. She was here with Peep last February.*

As I read, I am aware of other layers of misery which Meta leaves out. I now know so much more about her feelings towards her mother-in-law, and notice how she carefully doesn't say that *she* is looking forward to seeing Mrs Lender: *My mother-in-law is waiting for us very much.* Never at any time in her letters does she reveal how difficult she found Mrs Lender as a mother-in-law – yet this is something Mum could so easily sympathise with and respond to. The only oblique mention she ever allowed herself was in a September letter from Stocksund in 1947: *I don't want to live and work another winter in such a close room and so many people together. It is so very, very tiresome...* And the following month: *The children are nervous as well, when they can't be alone and undisturbed for a while.* What she didn't say was that the cause of some of her depression was Mrs Lender.

In my imagination, the first house where Meta and the children lived upon leaving quarantine was an ugly, cramped building in a mean street far from sunshine and trees. In reality it was a large, pleasant place on the top of a hill but a long way from any shops. The flat was small and very cramped – just a room with a kitchen alcove – and immediately below them was Mrs Lender, who had been there with Henno's sister, Ilka, and Peep since coming to Sweden two years before Meta and Henno. She complained constantly of the noise Meta made upstairs and told her not to walk about so much. Fortunately the children were only occasionally aware of the tensions, although they felt very shut in and restricted.

The landlord's daughter was kind to the girls, and Ann remembers how she took them on her bike for a breakneck ride down the hill. Ann was cautiously grateful for the kindness but clung on, voiceless with terror and screaming inside her head. She felt quite sure the brakes would fail, and braced herself for the crash and the pain – but, miraculously, they came to a safe stop. At the bottom of the hill was a park with trees and wide-open spaces. The walk back up was very tiring for little legs and for Meta, pushing Jaan and carrying shopping.

At first Mrs Lender read to them and talked to them often, so that Ann, who didn't remember her from their days in Estonia, grew to love her grandmother and the attention she gave them. But Meta had her own ideas about bringing up her children and felt diminished and criticised by Mrs Lender's constant interference.

As Ann grew older, she drew away from her grandmother and Aunt Ilka, realising just how badly they behaved towards her mother. They treated her not so much as an equal but as a servant, and Ann found it intolerable. She never discussed this with Meta, but by the time she was in her teens she had grown to dislike her grandmother intensely. In some ways she considered Aunt Ilka even worse when she learned of her reaction to Meta's safe arrival in Sweden after the traumatic flight from Estonia and the difficult two years in Germany. Instead of showing pleasure that her brother's family was safe at last, she scornfully asked Meta, "How on earth are you going to manage with your children?" Meta knew that Ilka feared they would impose on her or need her help, and she was not prepared to give them anything. She was also jealous of the possible demands they would make on her mother, whom she wanted to herself. At no time did she seem to acknowledge that it was thanks to Henno that she and their mother were alive and safe. On 19th September 1944, having sent his desperate message to Meta to flee the eighty kilometres to Pärnu, Henno had borrowed a car to race northwards to urge his mother and sister to get on any boat and escape. Without his somewhat foolhardy intervention they, like the other members of the family – including Ilka's husband – would have been deported and quite possibly would have died.

Mrs Lender was, admittedly, more generous-spirited. With typical determination and what Meta privately called her "awful will", she had from the outset decided to make as much as she could of her life in Sweden. She couldn't work as a teacher but was determined to prove to any of her former pupils who had survived that it was always possible to earn a living – always! When a job as a maid and housekeeper cropped up close by, she took it and set about mastering Swedish. Later she and other educated refugees were found office work, and she worked as an archivist in connection with school administration. All this is entirely admirable, but her brand of indefatigability left no room for emotion, which was obviously how she survived. Consequently she was totally lacking in empathy and understanding for Meta or even for her adored daughter, Ilka.

Meta felt her mother-in-law's criticism, both mute and voiced, every day and wasn't strong enough to fight it. She longed for encouragement, privacy and Henno's presence. It was all very well for Mrs Lender to talk about learning Swedish, but Meta didn't have much opportunity while she was at home looking after the children. On top of that, Mrs Lender had already been living in Sweden and working with Swedes for two years before Meta arrived in the country. Her intentions were plainly well meant but lacked empathy.

One evening, not long after their safe arrival in Stocksund, Henno arrived home bearing an enormous bunch of pink carnations as an anniversary present for Meta. It was a touching extravagance, and Ann was awed to see so *many* flowers. Meta laughed in delight, and the children and Henno joined in when she said there was no vase to put them in. From downstairs, Mrs Lender heard the commotion and, far from sharing their joy, was witheringly critical of Henno's waste of money.

There was a significance to those flowers beyond the immediate gesture of love, for Meta and Henno had chosen pink carnations for Meta's wedding bouquet. Mrs Lender, who'd had visions of Henno marrying a rich society lady and thought Meta a poor substitute, was scandalised by their bridal flower choice of pink. She was adamant that the bouquet should be *white*. "You could even have lilac from the garden," she'd observed acidly. But it was too late to change them, and Meta was reduced to tears. "The bride mustn't weep," Mrs Lender had snapped more than once, making Meta feel even more humiliated and effectively spoiling her day.

Mum didn't know any of this, and I still don't fully understand why Meta didn't confide in her. It's easy to see why she might not want to talk about it with any of her fellow countrywomen, because so many people only saw and admired the public face of Mrs Lender, and Meta was the first to admit that she was, in many ways, an admirable woman. But being her daughter-in-law was an altogether different proposition, and Meta had been dominated by her since childhood. She could surely have said something to Mum – or did she shrink from giving her something else to worry about when she was so obviously already full of concern for Meta? In her letters, Mum often told Meta that she was relieved for Meta that at least her mother-in-law and Ilka were nearby. Perhaps Meta had neither the heart nor the energy to correct Mum's idea of her relationship with Henno's family. Might it also have hinted at disloyalty to Henno? Certainly Meta didn't want that, so it was safer and less demanding to stick to news of the children, Henno and the wider world.

All my three children had measles during the Easter. Then I was again alone and Henno was a long way far. But all went normally and the children recovered quickly.

Many of Estonians in Sweden are going to Canada and USA. Some of them are quite pleased at their new homes, some of them are coming back to Sweden. We have no further plans. We don't want to leave Sweden. We hope we must not leave it before we go home. But where is our home? We refugees are people to whom a foreign land would never be a home and we are people whose old home is changed to be a strange one when we can go back. But still we must hope for the future and think of the children. Again, many thousands of our Estonian inhabitants are deported to Siberia and we know there is almost no possibility to see them again.

It is rather difficult to me to write in English and I am making mistakes. Swedish is going to disturb [confuse] me and I am not speaking English and I do read a very little in English – just there isn't much time for that. Perhaps next time it would be a little better. Now I am going to wait for your letter and news from your home.

11.10.49
Borås, Sweden

My dear Phyllis,

    Many thanks for your dear letter, where you told me all the news. I am glad for Hazel that she is well again and does like to go to school! I think it is the worst thing when children are ill. I feel myself so depressed when one of the children must be in bed. In the last summer all my three were well and were much out of doors. Now it seems to me that Jaan isn't quite strong this autumn. He has twice been unwell and has been indoors for a week every time. Especially his throat is aching. I am rather anxious about him. I don't know why he is catching cold so easily.

    We enjoyed our stay in Stocksund. The first ten days I was with Jaan alone and then Mai and Ann came from their holiday camp to Stocksund and we were there a week longer. We visited our friends and the time passed ever so quickly. Ann and Mai had really a lovely time at their holiday camp and they wish to go there next summer again.

    I am of course alone with the children. Henno is now in another place, not very far from us (three hours by train). Henno visited us last Sunday and maybe he is coming again after three weeks. It is hard to be separated, but I am glad that we are all together in Sweden and not in Russia. And Henno is coming enough and I needn't go to work.

    Henno's mother enjoyed to have all her four grandchildren staying with her. She is feeling rather well and doesn't keep off working. Peep is a big boy and a good pupil at school. He is very much interested in all sorts of sports and stamp collecting. Peep's mother [Ilka] has never heard anymore of her husband and we are sorry for that. She is working in a bank as a correspondent.

    I myself am rather alone in Borås, and there isn't much time to think of that.

    I remember so well your birthday party eleven years ago at your parent' home. I wish I could be with you on Saturday when you are going to have your Happy Family party. I wish you many happy returns of your birthday! With best greetings to your family and your parents with much love to you –

    From Meta

Speaking of Phyllis's family had reminded her of her time staying in England, and the next letter was not to Phyllis but to Nan:

17.1.50

Dear Mrs Shaw,

I am going to wish you a Happy New Year to you and Father Shaw. My regards to you and to Father Shaw come perhaps too late, but I say as we do in Estonian: It is better to do something late rather than not at all. And my children's best thanks to you for your nice Christmas present. That was really kind of you to remember my children and send them so funny books, I must tell them all about. I am glad to have the calendar you sent me. Oh many thanks. It is a pity the children can't speak English. I think next year Mai is going to take English lessons. In Sweden they begin to learn English in the fifth school year – I think it is too late.

We had this year a lovely Christmas time, because Henno was staying with us three days. We had a jolly Christmas Eve with the Santa Claus and many nice presents to everyone. Henno's niece was staying with us. She is living in Germany, now she got the permission to pay a visit to Sweden. During the Christmas she was with us in Borås, and now she is in Stocksund with Henno's mother.

Mai had a long holiday from December 21st until January 10th. Now she is enjoying to go to school again. Ann and Jaan started to go to kindergarten three hours a day every day. The kindergarten is only next door but one and they go there alone. They do like to go there and play with the other children. Ann is growing very big and she is bigger than Mai. I am sorry she couldn't go to school this year. She may begin in August.

We have today a lovely winter weather with sunshine. There is only too little snow. We had a few days ago thaw weather. Our climate in Borås is not very stable, and we have very much rain. It reminds me of staying in England.

I am now sending you and Father Shaw my friendliest greetings. With much love,
Meta

Until reading this letter I was unaware of how much Nan and Georgie

– Mrs Shaw and Father Shaw – still thought of Meta and cared about her. I realise now that Mum must have shown them her letters. I knew that Mum always sent a small present for them all at Christmas, but am strangely touched that Nan did too.

Eight months later Mum wrote:

20.08.50

My dear Meta,

You will think I have forgotten all about you as I have not written for so long. But I have not forgotten and think about your family very often. [...] I wonder how you and Henno and the children are and whether Henno is working far away.

I suppose the children have holidays from school now. Our children are due back at school on 5th September. Their holidays are passing quickly but they are greatly enjoying themselves. Just now we are staying at Twink's home in Frodsham. It is lovely country here. We are very high up and can look across to the Pennine Chain (a range of hills sometimes called the "backbone of England") and in the other direction we can see the wide estuary far away, where the river Weaver and the River Mersey flow together.

The weather is not very good for holidays, but we have been out quite a lot. We took the children to Chester Zoo last Friday and all had a happy time. [I remember that a goat in the children's corner ate my cousin Hilary's hair ribbon and nibbled off the end of one of her long fair plaits.]

One day last week we went to the coastal town of Llanfairfechan in N. Wales where Tony had been camping. [I have no idea how we got there, as we didn't have a car. Perhaps it was by train from Frodsham.] *Some of the little Welsh towns reminded me of some of the towns I visited with you and Henno in Estonia in 1939.*

You would hardly recognise Twink's boys, Michael and Tony. They have grown a lot since you last saw them! Michael is now 15 and Tony 13½. Hilary, their little sister is 6. She is 4 months younger than Hazel and they are having a lot of fun together. So are Peter and the boys. They have been out searching for butterflies. Peter is very interested in insects of all kinds and spends much time out of doors.

Hilary and I were very indignant sometimes when they excluded us, as they did when they went off on bike rides, lit a bonfire and cooked potatoes, or slept overnight in a tent in the field behind the house. Somehow the age gap between Pete and the boys didn't matter, but we were very much too young.

Rosemary is now 2. She is a happy little person and the children love her very much. She talks very clearly for her age and is very interested in picture books and pretends to read many stories.

What a terrible thing it is that so soon there is a war again in the world. It is so wrong that the fear of the shadow of war should always be present.

Write to me when you can and please forgive me that I have been so long writing to you.

My regards to Henno and love to the children and especially to you, my dear Meta.

Your affectionate,

Phyllis

It's the Korean War, 1950 to 1953, which she's referring to here, and I can just about remember it. Mum and Dad explained just a little of the situation to Pete and me, but were very protective of Rosa and took great care not to leave the newspaper about where she would see the photographs of war – and told us to do the same. At the time I thought it rather unnecessary, and it marked the beginning of many years of shielding Rosa from horrors – something almost inconceivable today with television and the Internet. She was the much-desired post-war child and it was as though they wanted to wrap her in cotton wool and protect her from all the atrocities and evils which punctuated the world's daily life. They later felt that their attitude had been unrealistic and perhaps harmful, but Mum in particular empathised so deeply with suffering that she didn't want her baby to be touched by it. I think now that she saw Meta in every anguished face and Meta's 'journeyings' unravelled in her head with every mention of the word 'refugee' – and this was difficult to live with.

For a while after the Korean War was ended, they quite seriously contemplated adopting a Korean child, and I was delighted with the idea. Of course, I simply imagined a delightfully foreign-looking baby who would be happy, smiling and totally adjusted to family life on arrival. I don't quite know why they didn't go ahead with an adoption; perhaps they considered the reality of coping with a traumatised child and felt they couldn't manage it. Whatever the reason, it became something else for Mum to feel guilty about.

Even though Mum didn't manage to write regularly, Nan kept in touch and filled Meta in on many details of family life. She was totally uninhibited and simply poured it all out with gay abandon and a liberal sprinkling of love and affection. Mum just couldn't do this. Meta was still very much her dear, dear friend, and because of this she felt deeply for her situation. She was appalled that Henno and Meta had to spend so much time apart; the anguish of her own, albeit minimal, separation from Dad never left her – and yet for Meta it was so much worse. She yearned to conjure a magic carpet and restore Meta to her family and a liberated home country. The reality was almost too painful to think about. How could she write cheerful, happy letters about her own life? I can't help wishing she had; Meta would have been glad for her. It was even more impossible to write about her problems. Again, I somehow wish she had for, without this sort of sharing, no friendship can continue to grow, and neither of them seemed to realise that. However, Meta's next letter was much more open. She was finding life difficult and suffered from fairly frequent migraine attacks, which were to continue for the rest of her life. Her depression was obvious:

3.4.52
Borås, Sweden

My dear Phyllis,
Many thanks for your letter. It is very kind of you to write to me, although I haven't written to you for nearly two years. I am glad you did write and told me all the news. I am often thinking of you and your children. I don't know why I haven't written to you. Time is just passing very quickly and there is always so much to do and I keep all my friends waiting so long for a letter. I don't feel myself very well, as I have often headache and I am tired. Perhaps I am so tired to be always alone with the children and there isn't anyone who would take care of them. When Henno is at home (he is coming every other weekend) he needs rest. And Henno isn't such a type of father who will play with the children. [My Dad was, of course, and perhaps Nan had told tales of his games in her lengthy letters.]

I am glad that your children have a happy home and they have a feeling of security. I am sorry to tell you that I haven't any feeling it is my home or it will be in the future. It is just living day after day and waiting for something else. The children are happier, they don't remember our real home and they don't feel they are strangers here. I am glad for that. Of course they are asking me sometimes – when [if] there will be a new war – where shall we go? When [if] the Russians come to Sweden – what will happen? I cannot answer because I dare not think of that. [Meta is possibly confusing the German 'wenn', which means 'if'.]

Mai and Ann are getting on very well at school. Next autumn Jaan is also beginning school. He has mumps now and I must keep him in bed. He is getting better now. I wanted to send you a little packet till [for] Easter, but now Henno is going to do that. It is easier for him in Tidaholm, [yet another placement] *as here in Borås the custom house is very far off and I must stay at home for Jaan's sake.*

You told me that spring is coming and you are working in your garden. We haven't any signs of spring. It is still very cold and it is snowing. It will be a very late spring in Sweden this year.

Mrs Lender is still in Stocksund and she is getting on quite well. She is going to have her 70th birthday in May. Her daughter and Peep visited us in last February. Peep has grown a lot since you last saw him. He is 13 years old and he is still at school (secondary school) and he wants to study some more years.

Mai and Ann learn to play the piano and they like to do it. My children are dreaming of their own house with a garden round it. We haven't just any garden and we are wanting it very much. Jaan is wishing to have a little pony. He is telling me that almost every day.

I hope your father is well again. I am going to wish you and your dear family a Happy Easter and a lovely spring time.

With much love to you and your children and to George. Many greetings to your Mother and Father.

Yours affectionately,

Meta

I don't remember this Easter package, but each time anything came from Meta I begged for a rerun of Mum's stories about her Estonia holiday. In my mind I created a vision of what it was like there: the buildings were amazingly beautiful, like castles fit for princesses; there were miles of wonderful sandy beaches, where children bathed naked; forests and flowery meadows were everywhere in all seasons; cream cakes and coffee were always accompanied by a glass of cold water – and the language itself was magical, with a simple item such as a safety pin called 'verdrukinnitusnöel'. But which of my friends believed any of this?

6.12.52
Borås, Sweden

My dear Phyllis,

Many days have passed since I received your dear letter. Thank you! I have often thought of you, but I haven't actually written any letter to you. But today I will write you a few lines telling you about our life here in Sweden.

We had a lovely summer because Henno was staying with us all the summer. Although the weather wasn't nice – we only had a fortnight nice weather and we could not bathe very much – we had a right [real] holiday. The schools started in the end of August. Jaan (he is now six years old) began in the first class. He likes to go to school very much. He can read and write and do the sums – he is very proud of course. Ann (she is nine) is going in the third class and she thinks that it is the most interesting thing to go to school. I am glad for that. Mai (11 years) started in the secondary school. She is learning English at school and has it six lessons a week. I try to help her in English as much as I can.

Henno is not in Borås. He has a place in Hallsbeg – a borough over two hundred kilometres from Borås. He is coming home every other Saturday afternoon. He is coming at Christmas time for two days. We are all very glad that he is able to come and stay with us. I am tired to be alone with the children and I feel that the children need to very much have the father as well. But we just can't do it otherwise – we have to wait.

My mother-in-law is in Stockholm with her daughter and grand-son Peep. Although she is seventy years old, she is still working and she wants to continue. She was staying with us for a week last August.

The winter has come very early this year. We had lots of snow and it is rather cold (-10 to -15c) I don't like to have it as cold as this, and the winter will be so long, so long.

Three days ago I sent you a little parcel. I hope you will receive it before Christmas. Perhaps you and the children will enjoy it. [It must have been chocolate.] *I wish that very much.*

Merry Christmas and a Happy New Year to you all from us all. Much love to your Mother and Father.

Your affectionate
Meta

More little parcels, more time passing. Mum often found life difficult, and constantly felt guilty about it. There was very little money coming in and she was depressed by the daily effort of making it last. We couldn't, for example, go to the penny slot machines in Croydon any more, or have a ride on the little, hairy Shetland ponies who walked around at the bottom of Kennards Arcade and sent me into ecstasies – there just weren't any pennies to spare.

As far as we children were concerned this made her cross, but we didn't understand that her anger wasn't directed at us. She wanted to be able to give us the moon, but it just wasn't possible. Like Meta, she suffered from migraines, and there seemed to be too many gloomy days when she had to lie in a darkened room. On those days *I* felt cross and let down by *her*. Sometimes I wanted to help, but my efforts often backfired – such as the time I washed my own hair under the fierce geyser in the bathroom and didn't realise that I'd flooded the floor in the process. Mum, with baby Rosa in tow, let fly such a torrent of crossness that I had towelled my hair completely dry by the time she'd finished. And I was only trying to help. Sometimes I wished she'd just smack us like other mothers did, instead of beating us with words.

Many things seemed to make her angry, and I often retreated to sit on the stairs to sulk or cry. The wallpaper there was brown and shiny, with an embossed pattern that tickled your fingers if you ran them over it. In places loose plaster trickled down behind the paper, and I wondered if the side of the house would fall down and kill me. She'd be sorry then!

And yet one part of me even then felt sad for her. I didn't understand her feelings, but I knew that, in some way, she didn't like herself. Sunday after Sunday I stood beside her at church and worried about the achingly forceful way she joined in with some of the service. "We have erred and strayed from Thy ways like lost sheep," she would say with heavy guilt. Even more worrying was, "We have left undone those things which we ought to have done…there is no health in us." It made me feel utterly helpless to hear my mother ranking herself with 'miserable offenders' and I longed to tell her it was all right. I think the seeds of my rejection of organised religion stem from those Sunday mornings. My intrinsically sunny nature, sulks on the stairs aside, rebelled against the emphasis on sin.

Mum was frequently depressed and disappointed. Her dreams of life as a family didn't match the reality, largely because of lack of money. Before the war, Dad's job in local government had appeared stable and not short of prospects – indeed, he was very lucky that it was held open for him after the war despite his conscientious objector status. But after the war the reality was very different. Though many jobs of this kind received reasonable pay rises, for some reason local government pay lagged far behind for many years. In 1965, the summer I graduated from university, I worked in Dad's office for a few weeks during my summer vacation. He was in the Motor Licence Department then and a severe backlog had caused them to employ a few temporary workers. Since I was planning to go back to university for another year, I wasn't interested when the boss offered me a permanent job. In fact, I was horrified and disgusted to learn that my potential salary, had I taken up the offer, would have started at a higher level than Dad's current earnings after more than twenty years of tedious graft and several promotions. He was third in seniority in a very large office, and that year his salary finally reached £1000.

Dad's sisters, my social worker aunts Mu and Joyce, used to admire Mum's ability to manage the housekeeping on around £5 a week and held her up to their clients as a paragon of virtue. She made many of our clothes, and Dad even made our sandals one summer, testing out skills he had learned in the army. We had an allotment close to the end of our garden and Dad worked hard to produce vegetables which we children weren't very keen on. Shopping for cheapness takes time, and Mum grew heartily sick of it. Dad toiled away and felt a failure for not bringing home more. But they were happy together and embraced the problems as a united couple.

In her most depressed moments, she used to bring herself up sharply by thinking of Meta. Ironically, Meta was financially fairly secure, but Mum didn't envy her this. What Meta had lost was beyond measure. Mum knew that she was lucky. She had not had to flee her home country, neither had she ever been parted from Dad for long during the war – and he hadn't been killed, which would have left her struggling even more. Furthermore, he came home to her every evening. She felt a heavy sense of failure at her inability to find all of this enough in itself.

Each Christmas she tried to send something that would delight Meta's children, and often spent more than she could afford. It seemed the very least she could do and was in some small way an expiation for the guilt she carried constantly about her dissatisfaction with life.

11.2.53
Trandaredsgatan, 28, Borås, Sweden

My dear Phyllis,

Many thanks to you for the books and the letter you sent me. The books for my children reached us just for Christmas – thank you very much. I have been naughty because I haven't written before. I translate these books for my children. Mai does not yet understand English so much that she could read them only by herself. But we are going to read them together and Mai will learn a lot by reading. Only the days are passing so quickly and the days at school are so long, so there isn't much time over to do many other things in the evening.

Henno was staying with us for two days at Christmas. We were all glad for that. We got our presents at Christmas Eve (on 24th) in the evening. We always do it like this. When the children were smaller Santa Claus used to come and give the presents to all, but he just cannot come any more – children like this sort of play with Santa Claus – I think we all like it. After Christmas we went to visit Henno in that place he is working. We stayed there for five days, and it was really a great change for us all. The children had three weeks holiday from schools. Now they are going to have a holiday for a week again – Swedish schools have their winter sports days. Many schools will go to the mountains (in Swedish fjäller) in the North Sweden for spring.

How did Peter manage his examinations? [This must have been the 11+.] *That is very kind of Hazel if she wants to write a letter to Mai. Mai says she cannot English but she will try to answer.*

We all think of those poor people in Holland who have lost their homes by that awful flood. That must have been horrible! We have great money collections to help these poor people. An exceptionally high spring tide and ferocious winds caused terrible flooding in East Anglia and Holland.

I exchanged a few short letters with Mai, three years older than me, but, like our mothers, we were not good correspondents and soon gave up. The age difference didn't help.

I found no letters for the three years which followed, although Meta and Mum may have written sporadically. Christmas 1955 evidently brought an exchange of gifts as always:

23.2.56
Borås, Sweden

My dear, dear Phyllis,

Many, many thanks to you and Mother Shaw for your presents to my children at Christmas. We were really surprised and Mai, Ann and Jaan were very pleased to get these things from England.

We had a lovely Christmas Day with Henno together. On Boxing Day he had to leave us again. But then we went to see him at his place (150 miles from Borås) and stayed there for ten days until the schools started again after the Christmas holidays.

It is really a very long time ago we last wrote to each other. I ought to have written to you earlier, but I haven't been very well. I have still awful headaches (migraine) and in some periods it is just worse and then I am not very energetic to write letters or do anything extra at all. There isn't much news in my life. Our life has not changed – only that the children are older and we ourselves are just older too. It is just the same – Henno is away – he has been at that place now over three years but he is still a temporary doctor there. We have got now Swedish citizenship and Henno has got the licence to be a district doctor. We now have to wait – either he gets this place where he is working now or he has to try in some other district. Only when he has got a constant place (I hope you understand me) we will be able to move into his flat or house (we don't know which one). We have no real family life and I am sorry for that. I feel sorry for Henno that he must be so much alone and I think our children miss him very much. I myself feel rather alone too, but there isn't much to be done and we have to wait still more.

Mai and Ann attend a Secondary School and Jaan is in the fourth form of the Elementary School. Mai will try to get into a High School this spring and Jaan must get a very good school certificate this spring in order to get into Secondary School. It is rather difficult here in Sweden to enter secondary or high school, there are too many pupils who want to – and they just can't take them all in – they have neither classrooms nor the teachers. I am quite anxious about them.

How are you and your family? How are Mr and Mrs Shaw? How is your sister's family? I should like to know about you. I am waiting for a letter from you and hope you will tell me all the news.

Will you please give my love to your children and George, to Mr and Mrs Shaw and your sister's family.

Mai, Ann and Jaan send their compliments.

Yours affectionately,

Meta

Mum was saddened to hear that Meta and Henno were still not settled together, since Henno had not, even now, found a permanent position. For the next couple of years there was little to tell each other, or to put into Meta's words: *There isn't much news in my life. Our life has not changed – only that the children are older and we ourselves are just older too.*

Small wonder that Meta was depressed, since for so many years she and Henno existed in a sort of limbo, never knowing when they would be able to settle somewhere together.

Ann and after

Mum's life wasn't entirely drab and inactive, though she knew what Meta meant. As the years passed she came to terms with herself and made a few friends, though none of them particularly close. By the time we children were in our teens she was a successful secretary to the women's group she belonged to at the church. In fact, she was so good at it that it was many years before she could pass the position on to anybody else. She grew and blossomed with the demands of the job, which involved letter writing, booking speakers and organising events for amusement, instruction and fundraising. There were plays to perform, choir concerts and parties. At one of the fundraising teas I, aged about ten, helped some of the women make sandwiches, and unwittingly mortified Mum by saying that we only ever buttered one slice before putting the unbuttered portion on top of the filling. This was, of course, an example of the economies practised in our house – and it would have been margarine, not butter.

Mum appeared in one play as a prison officer, and she had to spend much of the performance with a restraining hand on the prisoner's arm. Her every other line was "Don't be difficult". By the time of the performance this had become something of a family catchphrase, and I almost giggled aloud as we watched.

I was less controlled at the Christmas concert one year when a very red-faced lady, whom we naughtily nicknamed The Turkey, had several solo lines in the 'Boar's Head Carol'. "The boo-ors head, as I've hoo-eard tell," she warbled, hitting cascades of notes approximating to the tune. Both wobbly voice and face were too much for me, horrid child, and I had to depart to the

Ladies' in a fit of feigned coughing to get rid of my hysterics. Mum was not amused, but Dad was, and soon won her round.

Mum even began giving talks herself, initially because a booked speaker dropped out. It hadn't occurred to her before that she might have something to offer others from her small experience of life, because she spent so much time feeling ashamed of her lack of patience, tolerance and all the other Christian virtues with which she was obsessed. How often she said to me, "Oh Haze, what a horrible woman I am!" Dad was such an effortlessly good person; he didn't need to question things as she did, and always seemed to find redeeming features in his fellow humans. I don't know if he was aware that she always wanted to match up to him and was saddened by what she perceived to be her failures. She never seemed confident that he loved her as she was. What she failed to understand was that her very human frailties made her a sympathetic person. While Dad was understanding and helpful, she really empathised with others, and they appreciated it. Their shortcomings were hers too.

When I was about fourteen, Mum's name was put forward as a potential marriage guidance counsellor. She passed through the various selection hurdles and started her training with enormous enthusiasm. It was good to see her poring over books and pamphlets, busy with study that she obviously found interesting. She hadn't really got her teeth into anything so demanding since her Sunday School teaching days, when she'd studied child psychology and teaching methods from the book that she later sent to Meta. We got used to stumbling over piles of literature about marriage problems and teased her about her one-track reading. Dad was, at times, uncharacteristically irritated that marital problems held her in such thrall – I never fathomed why – but he enjoyed their expanding, interesting group of friends from among her fellow counsellors. Mum's confidence grew and at last she started to value herself a little.

We children weren't exceptionally aware at the time of how she was changing. Like most youngsters, we were pretty self-centred and found our parents as annoying and staid, as teenagers do. I remember Pete slamming out of a room shouting, "There's too much church and too little wine, women and song in this house." How I wished I'd dared say such a thing. Life was constantly 'not fair', and lack of money was often the source of disappointment. Whenever 'everyone' in the class had a skipping rope with wooden handles, or a penknife or whatever, we could rarely have one too. Of course, in reality neither could most of the class. Later, as our worlds expanded, Mum and Dad were always very strict about being home at whatever time they stipulated – always too early for our taste. However, in retrospect I realise how lucky we were. We had two united, very caring parents, an entirely adequate roof over our heads and no reason to complain of hunger.

Within the wider family Mum was very much a favourite aunt, as everyone knew she'd rather talk to them than do housework. "The dust will still be there tomorrow," she used to say – and it was.

For us it was an easy home to bring our friends into. From early on, our house had been the obvious social centre as we lived right opposite the primary school. It was assumed that our Mum would put up with activities that other mothers wouldn't like. One day she came home at the end of school time to find one of Pete's friends digging a large hole at the end of our garden. When she mildly asked what he was doing, he said their teacher had told them you'd find water almost anywhere if you dug deep enough – so he was trying it out and didn't think his Mum and Dad would let him do it in their garden. I suppose most parents would have been outraged, but Mum was both amused and flattered that he just knew she wouldn't mind. Before long there were several of us navvying away. We never did reach water, but we swore we could hear it trickling away out of reach.

Pete's secondary school was just a few hundred yards away, and he and his friends often spent their lunch hour at our house, eating their sandwiches to the accompaniment of their latest records or the strumming of someone's guitar. After school or at weekends many of my friends and Rosa's came to play or do homework, and Mum grew fantastically good at spinning out food so that it would stretch to feed a few extra mouths. Her bean dinners and soup meals were legendary and nothing like the sort of things we were offered at other houses.

Naturally we argued, grumbled and felt hard done by, like most youngsters; it must all be set down in the teenagers' union rule book. We didn't appreciate Mum and Dad's tolerance of noise, for example. Looking back, I recall how little fuss they made about both orthodox music practice or the jam sessions Pete and his friends loved in the era of skiffle groups. Then, when all the lads started being interested in air rifles, it was quite naturally in our garden that the targets were erected. More surprising was Mum's occasional participation.

My parents encouraged other hobbies over the years, from model making and needlework to the breeding of stag horn beetles. I can't now imagine where Pete sourced the grubs from but I remember the fascination at their repulsive peristaltic action viewed through the glass-sided box. They pupated in due course, then all chose to emerge from the chrysalis state and fly in at the bathroom window when I was in the bath. I could handle one beetle with its alarming horns but not a complete fly-past of learners who kept bumping into things, including me. My interests were all rather sedate by comparison, though I dreamed of becoming a famous actor or a trainer of guide dogs for the blind. The fact that we didn't even have a dog failed to stop me from being certain I would handle them superbly.

By the time I was eleven, finances had become a little less tight and my parents had been able to save enough to purchase the abandoned plot of land next door, with a view to building on it at some point in the distant future. Grandma, Dad's mother, had died a few years earlier, and Grandpa decided to sell the house in Guernsey where they'd planned to retire. He urged Dad to let him help finance part of the building, initially as a loan, to be offset from his inheritance later. They also needed a mortgage. We children were too young to be involved in the discussions and were totally surprised and excited when shown the plans of the new house. We'd never before seen a house being built, and found it amazing when lorries arrived laden with bricks, concrete, wood, window frames and so much else. It all grew far too slowly, but there came a day when we could go inside and see the downstairs areas, and I remember being allowed to climb a ladder and view the embryonic upstairs, which seemed an enormous space. We so enjoyed spreading out once we moved in and I was ridiculously pleased to give our new address to my form teacher – no longer number 18 but 20.

By the musical instruments and air rifle years, we had moved next door to the bigger house, and it had an extra bedroom, which was sometimes occupied by a paying guest. The money was a great help to our parents, and the people who stayed were a bonus as far as we children were concerned. There was a cousin of Dad's from Yorkshire who had moved to London for his job. Pete and I in particular really loved the way he treated us as adults rather than children. We were all rather regretful when he found a house and brought his wife and daughter south to join him. Then there was Jennie, the student daughter of friends, who was with us for a few months and seemed like a lovely older sister. After that there were foreign exchanges and a series of German assistant teachers, including Ailke, who became part of the family and is still a close friend. Another German teacher set fire to the spare bedroom by airing her undies too close to an electric heater.

In 1960 Mum was thrilled to hear news from Meta after a long silence. Not before time, Henno had found a position as a GP not far from Uppsala, and they were at last together as a family. Furthermore, Meta had finally made contact with her mother and brother in Estonia; amazingly, both had survived the war and were well. It had taken twenty years to discover that they were still alive.

I scarcely registered this fantastic news. More exciting as far as I was concerned was the request that Ann, Meta's second daughter, might come to stay with us to improve her English. Mum was delighted: *We shall be very happy to have Ann to stay with us if she would like to come. I have always hoped that even if you and I could not meet again, some of our children would be able to.* She was anxious, though, about the lack of space in the house, as we already had my German penfriend coming for six weeks. *Now I wonder whether Ann would mind sharing a bedroom with our daughters? Unfortunately our income is not very great, so would it be possible to ask you to pay £1.10s.0d. each week for food?* Oh Mum! What did it cost you to write that last bit? You must have hated it, but it really was necessary. Many years later, I learned that Meta was shocked that Phyll asked so *little*.

And so began a wonderful, enduring friendship for me. How awful it would have been if Ann and I had hated each other on sight and felt obliged to make all the right noises for our mothers' sakes! Fortunately we liked each other very much.

Ann came shortly before I finished my O level exams, so in the weeks that followed I was fairly free, though we still had to go to school. Sometimes Ann came too and she amazed us with her immensely good English. Most of my close friends were used to feeling cheerfully inferior about foreign languages, as we'd seen our friend Judy, a Hungarian refugee, learning to come to terms with English and master it in four years. Not only that – she'd kept up with the majority of the other subjects, including two more languages, German and Latin. What was it about 'foreigners' which made them so enviably good at languages?

Judy's mother was very keen to meet Ann and compare notes about how Meta coped in a strange country. There are similarities between the Estonian and Hungarian languages. I listened, fascinated, to Mrs Vajda's questions and came much closer to understanding the isolation of the refugee and the yearning to go back home. They were soon in tears. Until then I suppose I had found it a rather romantic idea to escape from persecution to a safe place. The story of Meta's biblical flight from Estonia had glowed inside me since early childhood. But not any more. As Mrs Vajda talked in her faltering English, I felt her sense of loss. Judy had always made light of their escape to the West, but her mother made me glimpse the fear. For Ann this was familiar territory. She didn't remember much of their journey from Estonia, although she did recall some details of their arrival in Sweden. But she was very used to the sense of anxiety and not belonging.

I couldn't imagine what it must feel like not to belong. I had a well-defined place in a secure family in a safe country which I liked well enough – it hadn't occurred to me not to. It made me think back to the six weeks spent with a French family the year before and try to imagine what it would have been like not to come home. The very idea gave me the shudders, as I'd hated it. It wasn't just that the language was different; the whole flavour of the place – coloured solely by the family I stayed with – its culture, outlook and values were not what I was used to. But Ann and Judy were adapting to all these things. How I admired them!

Mum was clearly thrilled to have Ann there and they talked endlessly about Meta, Estonia and Ann's family. Mum couldn't hear enough, but found much of what Ann told her very sad. Meta's health had suffered, and her frequently severe headaches didn't respond to treatment. The letters had suggested that much of Meta's vivacity had been dimmed, and Ann could only confirm this. Life for them in Sweden was materially good, but they yearned for their roots and their own people. They appreciated the kindness of the Swedes for taking in so many refugees, but felt they lacked understanding since Sweden hadn't known war and its sufferings at first hand. Many Estonians clung to their language and traditions, always hoping to return one day. Ann's family was no exception. They were brought up as Estonians in Sweden. "I could never marry a Swedish boy," Ann told me.

It's difficult to recall what we did for those ten or so weeks, but we certainly talked and often laughed. My glamorous German friend, Birgitt, felt somewhat excluded, as Ann seemed like part of our family whereas she was just a visitor. We girls certainly did things together, but Birgitt and Ann didn't really get on very well. Ann's English was excellent when she arrived and even better by the time she'd been with us for a few weeks. She quickly became like an extra daughter in the family – a much more helpful one than

I was – and even called my parents "Mum and Dad".

Nan and Georgie welcomed her as a grandchild but were more reserved with Birgitt, a German, of course, though a blameless 16-year-old. Nan in particular was ecstatic at seeing Ann, and recounted memories of Meta's stay. We went quite often to 169 for tea, so Ann was able to see the house where her mother had been so happy. I still privately thought the whole area where they lived was extremely ugly and always found the road long and boring. Ann was more mature than me and recognised that it was not so much the place as the people who had so delighted her mother.

By then Twink, Alan and family had moved from Cheshire to a house a mile away from us, so Ann was able to put yet more names and faces together. Meta wouldn't have recognised Michael, now married and with a home of his own, and Tony, now twenty-three and a teacher, although still living with his parents. Hilary had initially stayed with friends in Cheshire to do her O levels but was going into the sixth form with me.

Once the school holidays began, the next few weeks just evaporated. We managed trips to London, which was as unfamiliar to me as to them, even though we lived so near. I don't know to this day how Mum and Dad scraped together the train fares. We girls and Mum spent a sunny week near Chichester in a delightful little cottage belonging to a friend of Auntie Joyce. It was a low-ceilinged place with beams and a steep staircase leading to two minute bedrooms on the first floor. From the linen basket-sized landing was a fixed ladder and a thick rope handrail to an attic room where Rosa and I slept. The garden too was idyllic, with roses rambling around the porch and delphiniums and clarkia everywhere. It certainly gave Birgitt and Ann a taste of rural England at its most picturesque, and we loved it too. Mum was in her element there; for her it was Forge Cottage all over again, but with many more conveniences. She amazed us all with her ability to name flowers and birds, so it wasn't just Ann's and Birgitt's vocabularies that grew. I wished she could always be as relaxed and happy as this. It hadn't occurred to me before how hemmed in she felt by the suburbs.

Having Ann with us made Mum a different person. I suppose Rosa and I could have felt very jealous of Mum's devotion, but we didn't. Ann's presence made Mum's stories of Meta come alive. We'd always believed what she told us, and I'd enjoyed embroidering the details in my imagination. But here was someone from that story, and I was intoxicated by the way our two families had a sort of shared mythology. Ann too had been brought up on stories of Meta's time in England and Mum's time in Estonia as well. It was like fitting together a marvellous jigsaw puzzle which expanded and became more detailed the more you placed the pieces.

All too soon Birgitt went back to Germany, but I would see her the following summer when I went to stay with her family for a very happy seven weeks. Twink came home from work to find a note from Tony: "Gone to Germany, back soon." He'd roared off in hot pursuit of Birgitt, whose rather surprised family put him up for a few days before urging him to return for the start of his new school term. He was, after all, a teacher now. I often wonder how many other broken hearts littered Birgitt's wake.

As Ann's departure drew near, we all felt depressed, Ann included. She'd become so very much part of the family. We couldn't afford to go and see her in Sweden and didn't know if she'd be able to come back. Through her, my very sheltered world had expanded.

I don't remember seeing Ann off but I do remember tearful goodbyes and a great sense of loss. We promised to write, but it wasn't going to be the same, and we knew it. For Mum it was a hard departure too. She'd come closer to Meta again through Ann and didn't want to let go of this closeness. Ann had been a wonderful companion to *her* too. Mum wrote to Meta just a few hours after Ann left. I do hope I was aware of her sense of loss at the time, but I'm afraid I was too preoccupied with my own.

16.8.60
Wallington

My dear Meta,

It was very hard to let Ann leave and come home to you! We love her very much and she is really one of the family Parkinson. We shall miss her very much indeed now she is gone and we wish she could stay longer. What a dear, dear daughter you have! Thank you for letting us borrow her these last weeks and please let her come back to us another time. Perhaps you could come with her then?

We have tried to do as many different things as possible to make Ann's stay here a happy one – and she in turn has been so helpful and 'at home' with us.

We are sorry to know that you are still troubled by your headaches and do hope that your last stay in hospital will have proved a good one – that the doctors will have found a way to treat the cause of the headaches. Good health is such a precious thing and I do hope you will feel much better soon. We have talked about you all so much and feel we know so much more about your way of life now.

Thank you for the lovely wooden horse you have sent for me and for all the other little gifts for the family. The horse is standing on the bookcase in our sitting-room and I see him every day. I am sending for you the little marmalade house that Ann fell in love with and I shall imagine it on your meal table sometimes. I am sending it for you with my dear love.

My mother and father are so happy to have seen Ann and feel it quite wonderful that after all the events of the last twenty years they should be able to meet and love your daughter.

The horse was a wooden one about the size of a cat, painted red with swirls of other colour, a traditional design from the Daler region of Sweden. All Mum's grandchildren enjoyed it in later years and it's now treasured by Rosa's youngest daughter.

Greetings and love to you all from all our family and very much love to you, dear Meta.
Your affectionate,
Phyllis

She wrote quickly to Ann too – I'm certain I didn't. Ann's reply was equally prompt:

19.8.60
Alunda, Sweden

My dear 'Summer-Mum',
Thank you very much for the letter I got today. It is so nice to hear from you so soon. I really don't feel to be so far away from you then.

First of all I must thank you very, very much for the marvellous time I had with you. When I think of it, I just wish it had not gone so quickly. But we shall meet soon again I hope and I shall try to take my mum with me. Just now it doesn't seem that impossible for when

I came home and told her about you, she really seems to long for you all. So just wait — we'll come soon!

It was of course very nice to see all our family again. I'm just waiting for my sister — she is coming home tomorrow evening and then the whole family will be together again!!

Once more very many thanks and love to all of you from
Ann
XXXXX (one for each of you)

A month later came a letter from Meta:

16.9.60
Alunda, Sweden

My dear Phyllis,

Thank you so much for your kind letter and the marmalade house that Ann likes. I like it too and we use it sometimes on our breakfast table. Many thanks to you and your family for my birthday greetings. It was a very pleasant surprise for me.

I do apologise for the long delay in writing to you, but have had much to do since Ann came home. Two days after Ann arrived Mai came home from Germany. She came together with Henno's cousin [...] a lady over seventy. We had not seen her for fourteen years. She was staying with us over a week and then Henno took her to Stockholm to his mother. Now she is back in Germany again. She was very pleased to see us all after so many years. She was in Sweden for the first time and did a lot of sightseeings in Stockholm.

The schools started in the end of August and I think it is quite troublesome to get it arranged for the girls, who have to go to Uppsala. Mai is studying German language and, in the beginning, she seems to be contented. Mai is living in Uppsala (the girls have a room there) and she comes home only over the weekend. Ann comes home some days and stays in town sometimes. It depends how much homework she has and how long the school day lasts. But she loves to come home.

A fortnight ago I got a bad cold. I catch cold very easily and I think it is very annoying. It is so difficult for a housewife to be ill in bed and many things stay undone waiting you to be well again.

Ann and me are often talking about you and your family. I cannot say how thankful I am you allowed Ann to come and stay with you. She had a most wonderful time and a very different time. She loves family life and to come into contact with people. We are such a small family in comparison with yours. That makes a difference. We don't feel at home and the children feel almost the same. But in England when Ann was staying with you, she saw a real family life with other young people coming and visiting you and yourselves going to other families and feeling at home. And all the time Ann had a feeling that she was belonging to your family and felt the friendship and warmth and love. I don't know how to explain it, but I hope you understand me. We Estonians here are missing our relations and friends. With the Swedes we just cannot get the right contact and we haven't much in common.

Ann was so unhappy leaving you and England, because she felt herself really like a member of your family. She has told me so much about you all and other people she met there, that I almost feel I have seen you.

Henno has not had his holidays yet. It is very difficult to get a substitute. But we still hope to get a doctor who will come here instead of Henno for some weeks. We have had a warm and lovely week now with much sunshine and no rain at all just before a long dark autumn. I don't like winter – it is too cold for me with lots of snow and the days are so short. But everything is passing too quickly and you just cannot manage all you wish.

Greetings to you from all our family and much love to you,
Your Meta

With this letter, the sparkle of Ann's visit dimmed. Mum was saddened to realise how much the war years had changed Meta, and she wanted to rush off to Sweden to make everything better. She often thought of the future they'd talked about as young women. They had both wished for their own homes and children, but for Meta there never really was a family home, since Henno's settled country practice didn't begin until Mai and Ann were leaving for at least part of the week. Mum felt this deeply. It also made her dread the fact that our family was reaching a stage when it would naturally fragment. Pete was about to go to college and I hoped to do the same a couple of years later, although Rosa would be at home for some years yet. Mum told me once that from the time we could walk, she'd consciously schooled herself to accept that one day we'd go away. The idea was so ghastly that she had to rehearse it for years, while at the same time she wanted us to have our independence and be happy.

Meeting and parting

Ann and I wrote to each other in a haphazard way over the next couple of years, but we were both very engrossed in our schoolwork. She was planning to follow in her father's footsteps and become a doctor, while I wanted to study English and be a teacher. We both lived very full lives and understood that there wasn't much time or inclination for letter writing. Our relationship was already so close that we were certain that it would endure no matter how little we knew of the ephemera of our separate lives; we would be able to pick up just where we had left off. All of this proved true.

In the summer of 1962 Ann came again. It merges now in my mind with the first visit, simply a comfortable memory of relaxation, laughter and talk followed by more talk. But I do remember noticing that Ann had changed a little. Whereas before she had clung to her Estonian roots, now she wanted to be more Swedish, more fully integrated with her adopted country. She was aware that her parents still hoped to return to Estonia one day but she wasn't so sure any more that this was a particularly good idea – at least for herself. I took delight in teasing her because she was no longer adamant about marrying an Estonian boy.

I was struck too by her independence. For a long time she and Mai had been fending for themselves during the week when they lived in the flat in Uppsala, and latterly Ann hadn't gone home to Alunda at weekends. She was already branching out on her own. In theory I was ready to do the same, but knew I wasn't going to find it as easy as Ann.

Mum loved having Ann again and couldn't hear enough about Meta. Ann and I had immediately slotted back into an easy friendship and we didn't find it quite so hard to part this time, as we were sure we would meet again. But for Mum it marked the beginning of several partings which she'd been dreading and found hard to bear. For two years Pete had been unable to get a 'living in' grant. He was studying in London and the county, providers of the grants, considered it close enough for him to live at home. He'd found it very difficult to be a student and still live at home; it was so restricting for several reasons. Although we lived relatively near two railway stations, the trains didn't always run late enough for him to do what he wanted in London. As a student at the Royal College of Art, he often had unwieldy portfolios to cart around and three-dimensional pieces of work that didn't travel well on public transport. And, of course, it was a disaster for his social life. Having seen the problems he encountered, I'd decided to apply to universities a long way away to avoid suffering the same kind of dual existence. I also recognised that I would find it quite difficult to leave home, and forced myself to do it thoroughly.

While Ann was with us this second time, Peter finally received a grant which enabled him to live near college for his third and fourth years. Having just completed my A levels, I expected to be off to university too, meaning that the two of us would leave home at the same time. Therefore, Ann's departure was a symptom of radical changes in Mum's home life. I learned later that she, Dad and Rosa all found those first few months without us very depressing. Yet she could write quite bracingly to Meta about it:

Life has been very different for us this term with both Peter and Hazel away. Rosemary, George and I have found it rather strange and a bit melancholy sometimes. However, it is good that they are so happy in their work and that is the thing that really matters.

Mum, why don't you say to Meta how you really felt, how desolate and weighed down? I suppose you wanted to protect her from your unhappiness – or did you feel that she hadn't complained about losing Mai and Ann so you should be stoical too? It saddens me that you hid so much from each other – something Ann and I have tried not to do.

Quite suddenly and miraculously, in 1965 Meta came to England for a holiday. We knew Ann had been trying to persuade her to come ever since her own first stay with us, but it always seemed most unlikely. She and Ann planned to be in London for a week, but Meta was strangely unsure whether Mum would want to see her. Mum's response was immediate and unequivocal:

My dear Meta,

This is a very short note to say YES OF COURSE WE WANT TO SEE YOU! when you are in London.

What made Meta so hesitant? She surely couldn't have doubted Mum's continued affection. No, I'm sure it wasn't that at all. Perhaps she felt that since they hadn't met for more than twenty-five years, it was better to keep their memories of that idyllic time, to polish those mutual images rather than face their present selves. Possibly too it was unendurably painful to remember her old life in Estonia.

At this time Mum was working part-time as a secretary in a childcare office, Rosa was at school and I was on holiday from university, so on their first morning Meta invited me to have coffee with her and Ann in the roof garden of Derry and Toms. It was strange meeting Ann in such opulent surroundings, and despite being a self-opinionated and seasoned student I was rather intimidated and oddly overawed by Meta. She seemed so dignified and controlled. I don't know what I expected, and had at this time not read any of her letters to Mum, merely basing my knowledge of her on the stories fed to me over the years and Ann's description of her. The face was familiar from the photos, but I didn't know how to cope with the actuality of someone so very precious to Mum and so unknown to me.

I think too that I was forcibly brought up against the fact that this poor refugee family was financially far better off than we were. For us, there was never any question of eating out in London, not even to the extent of coffee and cake. On the few occasions we went to a museum or went sightseeing with foreign visitors, we took sandwiches and a flask. Eating out was restricted to a very occasional cup of tea and bun in Croydon, or the fish and chip lunch which Nan used to treat us to in half-term holidays when we were young enough to enjoy meeting her from the shop. As a student I wasn't in the habit of spending much of my grant on entertainment. Yet there I was in a very expensive store, drinking coffee and eating pastries far more sophisticated than I'd met before. And to Ann and Meta this seemed relatively normal. Was Meta too very conscious of this discrepancy in our experiences, and did she fear it could get in the way of her friendship with Mum? I know from Ann, as I've written before, that Meta was astonished at the modest amount Mum had asked her to pay for Ann's board on her first visit to us – surprised, but acknowledging that it was essential. With more maturity I came to see that the happiness and security of my home was of far greater value than the ability to eat in restaurants.

With greater maturity and also knowledge.

Much more relaxed was a large family picnic in the Surrey countryside which included Nan and Georgie, 'Mother and Father Shaw'. Nan and Meta smile at me from a photograph taken then; Meta's arm is around Nan, who looks dazed and ecstatic. In these surroundings I warmed to Meta and looked fondly at Nan as she kept grasping Meta's hand and gazing at her as though she might disappear in a puff of smoke.

Nanny with Meta

But of Mum and Meta there is no photo. They must have met privately between Derry and Toms cakes and coffee and this picnic, but I don't know where or when, and neither does Ann. It should have been a momentous occasion – it was the climax of so many years of friendship and letter writing – but Ann and I know nothing about it at all. Was there everything or nothing to talk about? I never thought to ask Mum until now, when it's too late. I'd love to describe it as a high point in both their lives, a magical moment which recharged such an enduring and important friendship. For all I know it was just as I imagine.

Now I should love to think that from then on Mum wrote much more freely to Meta and confided in her. There are small signs of this. In the autumn of 1967, following a sudden brief visit from Ann, she wrote:

Perhaps Ann will have told you that I have – or rather George and I have – two children living with us, Howard 15 and Manya 13. They are two of the five children of George's youngest sister, Christine, who took her own life in April. They are supposed to be here just for a year – but whether it will be longer I don't know. They have fitted in very well really but I must say I find it difficult at times. I don't really want to make the effort to look after the needs of two youngsters like this – but I do my best mostly!

But so much is left unsaid. She doesn't even mention how traumatic she found it to be left on her own for a few weeks while Dad went off to Canada to sort things out with Christine's husband and the children. As it happened, I was on my own too as Henry, my husband of ten weeks, was leading an expedition of boys in Iceland at the time. Mum came to stay with me at our flat and we cheered each other up as best we could. Rosa was away at college and I was in my first year of teaching and didn't have much time to mope, but Mum spent hours alone trying to quell the emotions that had been stirred up from long ago during the war. She'd rarely been parted from Dad since then and was also struggling to sort out her feelings about being a mother again, and was not altogether sure how she would cope. Both she and Dad questioned how appropriate it was to bring the children out of their familiar environment and away from their other brother and sisters. Howard and Manya were coming to relatives they scarcely remembered and to a country they didn't know at all. Meta might have had helpful comments about this.

In the same letter she mentions that Rosa was now at college but hadn't settled in very well. What she failed to mention, either here or in earlier letters, was that Rosa, the peacetime child so much cherished and desired, had sadly developed a psychiatric illness. During the previous summer, before I'd started teaching, I'd helped Mum and Dad nurse her through an appalling few weeks which I've never forgotten. Both of my parents suffered incredible bouts of guilt and despair, feeling their treatment of Rosa may have had something to do with her condition, despite the fact that the doctors involved assured them that this was not in any way relevant. Meta never knew any of this.

My greater insight puts a completely different emphasis onto the fact that all wasn't well with Rosa at college – and to Mum's mixed feelings about having a nephew and niece to stay for so long. She and Dad had been through such a terrible time just before Christine's suicide – a suicide triggered by recurrent psychiatric illness. Was Rosa destined to suffer in the same way? Meta would have sympathised so readily with all this. It might have been salutary for her to see that life wasn't smooth for Mum despite her settled home and loving family. Ann and I didn't write often during our student years as our lives were so fully occupied. We sent birthday and Christmas greetings, but little news. Had I told her then about Rosa and my Canadian cousins, as I certainly did much later, she might have passed the news on to Meta.

All the rest of Mum's letters to Meta from 1967 to 1981 were unfailingly warm and consistently cheerful. She told of our marriages and the arrival of each new grandchild; she reported on Nan's and Georgie's health until their deaths. She lightly touched on Dad's heart attack in 1974, from which he made a good recovery, but said nothing about her own feelings when it happened or later. She completely left out any mention of her own health. By 1969 she was almost housebound and in constant pain from a severely arthritic hip that had deteriorated badly over four years. The day before our son was born in 1969, she had a hip replacement operation – and, at the same time, poor Rosa was back in a psychiatric ward. Meta never knew any of this.

Christmases and birthdays continued to be marked with cards. Mum charted our various house moves and finally their own when Dad retired. She made no mention of holidays or of her second hip replacement. She also gave no sense of greater ease as their financial situation became increasingly good with each successive year. Those letters contain no real emotion at all. Yet Mum was such an emotional person.

In October 1981 Dad died. At Mum's request, Pete wrote to tell Meta:
Just a note to tell you the sad news that my father, George, died suddenly last Thursday night. He had been fit and well and his death was quite unexpected. Typically, he had been laying bricks for a house extension he was building, then in the evening he took part in a performance of a play, attended the party afterwards and collapsed and died as he was getting into his car.
Mum has taken it very well and is staying with us for a while. She was concerned that I should write to you since you had known them both for so long.

I know what Pete meant by *Mum has taken it very well* – but really the reverse was true. She never got over his death, however apparently calmly she appeared to take it at the time. His last day, she told me, was a very happy one for them both, with no trace of irritation. He was busy with the extension, and she planted bulbs in the garden for much of the afternoon, so they chatted companionably as they worked away. When she straightened up after planting the last bulb, she was taken aback to find herself wondering whether Dad would see them come up in spring – but dismissed the idea as nonsense and went in to put the kettle on.

Just a few weeks before, on an unbelievably warm sunny weekend in September, Pete's family and ours joined forces to help Dad with the foundations of the little extension. At nine, ten, eleven and fifteen, the four grandchildren were old enough to be really useful – and to enjoy it. After some trial and error, we sorted ourselves out into a continuous chain of shovellers, emptiers and barrowers, with the unskilled labourers feeding the hired cement mixer and carting the results to the trenches, where the more skilled workers slapped and smoothed the mixture into place, coaxing it into corners and embedding pipes in the right position for the loo that would be installed later. It was a messy, satisfying business, with plenty of laughter and fooling around. At intervals we paused for drinks and sandwiches, surveying the progress with pride. Dad was in his element.

It had all gone so well that by the evening there was nothing more to do, and we all decided to make the most of the last little bit of summer and go to the coast for the day. We found a nearly deserted stretch of sandy beach not far from Climping on the south coast and had a gloriously restful day in and out of the water. One of the children found a piece of cowl-shaped piping, which made a most successful hearth for a beach barbecue; we've always had a passion for cooking sausages over driftwood fires. Dad took his last photos there, as we discovered months later when Mum finally had the film developed.

I remembered that weekend as I drove over to Mum's the day after Dad died, and was distracted to notice the state of the extension. Dad had laid several courses of bricks, enough to put the external door frame in place, propped by a spare piece of wood. To me it seemed oddly symbolic that here was an empty doorway, leading nowhere or everywhere depending on how you looked at it. It was as though Dad had just stepped through to – what?

I'm glad they spent such a good final day together, because sometimes Mum was rather bad-tempered with Dad. Though she loved being in a country village again after so long, she missed her marriage guidance work, which had given her such a sense of self-worth – and, of course, the very good friends she had made there. Dad had slotted so well into country retirement and found a real niche for himself, but she wasn't as occupied as he was, and resented his placidity and easy involvement with things which didn't necessarily include her. Almost in anticipation of the forthcoming years without him, she'd wanted to monopolise his time. For months after they moved she had felt quite lonely, despite visits from friends who envied their retired state. At the same time she felt her usual guilt about her behaviour and feelings.

Fortunately, by the time Dad died she was beginning to find her feet in the neighbourhood and make good friends. They'd both become part of the local parish church community, finding it more to their taste then the little Methodist Chapel, and got on well with the vicar and his wife. Knowing Mum's former link with marriage guidance, the vicar involved her in bereavement counselling, and she'd thoroughly enjoyed the various training sessions and the people she met there. It's ironic that the area of concern was bereavement, although it did lead her to firm friends who were a great support after Dad's death.

In the evening of his last day, the one before I stood looking through the empty doorway, Dad went off to act in his play and Mum stayed in the village to give a talk at a meeting. She had seen Dad perform the previous night. She hadn't expected him back particularly early as there was to be a party after this, the last night, so wasn't alarmed until the phone rang at about midnight. The call was from a policeman, who wanted her to give him directions to her home. He refused to say why he was coming, but Mum guessed at once that something was wrong and met him on the doorstep, angrily demanding to know what had happened to Dad. By this time the young man – and he was very young – was aghast at how he'd mishandled the situation, and it was he, rather than Mum, who needed the hot sweet tea.

Pete and his family lived less than a mile away, so she wasn't on her own with the policeman for long. She and Pete went to identify the body in the early hours of the morning, and she told me how she'd wanted to stay with Dad longer. She would have liked to be left alone with him, but the sympathetic officials obviously thought that it would spare her pain if the formalities were swift. Dad was still warm to the touch and very peaceful, apart from a bruise on his cheek where he'd hit himself on the bonnet of the car as he fell. All she said as she stroked his face was, "Poor old chap."

Neither then nor later did I see her cry. I so wished she would. I think with Rosa she may have done at some point. The only time I was able to hug her in shared grief came several years after, when she was only a few months from death herself. I was visiting her in the nursing home and very aware on this particular day that she had slipped a little further away from reality. She wasn't very talkative, but suddenly looked at me very calmly and said, "Do tell me, Haze, because no one else will. Is Daddy dead?" I was shocked by the question. How long had she been wondering? Was she upset that he hadn't visited her? How much did she now remember of her surroundings? I managed to tell her that yes, Dad had died. She seemed satisfied as she said, "I thought so," and we wept a little together. I had to contain my greater grief until I reached the car and drove home, as I didn't want her to be concerned about *me*. Perhaps, I now wonder, it would have helped her if I hadn't been so restrained.

It was not until a later visit that I mentioned the conversation to the matron. Apparently there was a young nurse in the home called Georgina, mostly shortened to 'George'. Mum must have heard her name called through the house by other nurses, and her poor confused brain thought it was *her* George they were calling. I'm glad I cried with her then, but wish I could have done so years earlier.

Like many a funeral, Dad's was a strange mixture of pain and pleasure. It was typical of Dad's accommodating nature that he'd died just before the school half-term holiday, since we children were all involved in education, Rosa's husband being a teacher too. Rosa and her family came down from York and spent a whole week with Mum, and Pete's family and ours lived sufficiently near to be there often. Many relatives and friends came from all over the country, and it was good to see them; they all shared the idea that Dad's way of dying was, for him, a wonderful way to go, despite the shocking suddenness. It would not have been easy to see him decline into feeble old age, since he was always so active and full of life. But he was only sixty-eight, and it seemed as though he'd been cheated of a few more years.

Mum had asked for donations to the National Children's Home rather than flowers, since Dad so hated waste of any kind. Grandpa, his father, had been involved with the organisation throughout his working life, and Dad had continued the connection. The only flowers were from Mum, and it was my job to arrange this for her. She wanted a spray of red roses like she'd had in her wedding bouquet, but later asked me to amend the order so that there were forty-two blooms – one for each year of their marriage – though the last year was incomplete.

Meta naturally wrote to Mum after the news of Dad's death reached her, and Mum responded:

27.11.81
Headley Down
Hampshire

My dear Meta,

Thank you for your dear letter – George had not been ill – he was well and active but died suddenly and at once of a heart attack. If he had to go then we are so glad he did not have to suffer.

The children and grandchildren are being such a help and comfort to me and I feel cared for and supported. We had over 41 years of married life during which we loved one another and understood each other more and more. Nothing can take all that away – it's just I have to get accustomed to the fact that George's presence is no longer with me.

I am so glad that all is well with you and Henno and that you have pleasure in your children and grandchildren. They give one great joy.

With my love to you and Henno,
Phyllis

She never wrote a letter to Meta again.

Sweden

On a beautiful day in 1989 I flew to Stockholm. For months I'd pored over books about Estonia, re-read Meta's letters to Mum, which I'd found when clearing the house after she died – and tried to piece together my half-formed ideas for this book. Henry, my husband, and I talked about it often. Over lunch one day when I was outlining my latest thoughts, it suddenly struck me how little I really knew about Meta. What if she didn't like the idea of my writing about her? Suppose she objected to my seeing her letters? Would she hate it if I raked up the past? "Well, go and ask her," Henry said. Such a simple idea just hadn't occurred to me.

A simple idea it might have been, but it took many months before I could get everything organised. By now Henry and I had left teaching and were trying to start a small guest house business on Dartmoor, so my timing had to fit in with existing bookings. Added to that, my letter asking Ann if she'd make the first approach to Meta had arrived when Ann was out of the country, and, as in the best of households, it had been tucked away by one of her children and forgotten about. For weeks I waited for a response, and began to feel very despondent as such a long silence could only mean that Meta disapproved. Then finally, when I'd almost given up hope, I had a phone call from Ann. She had just discovered the letter and was horrified to think how long I'd waited in suspense for a reply. The good news was that Meta was quite happy for me to write about her and use the letters; she was baffled that I thought them useful or interesting, but happy just the same. And Ann was delighted that I was at long last thinking of taking up her standing invitation to come and stay.

Dates were fixed for months ahead; everything finally fell into place and I was on the plane. Not being a very good traveller, I'd taken the precaution of swallowing the relevant anti-sickness pills well in advance. Once we'd taken off and negotiated a sharp, stomach-churning right turn above Gatwick, I began to relax and enjoy the flight. Our meal arrived almost at once and my fellow passengers, a group of Swedish people returning from a conference in London, all burst out laughing. Apparently they'd all been rather pleased to learn that the hotel would serve breakfast in their rooms that morning – until the insipid, plastic-wrapped meals arrived. The airline food was identical down to the last detail.

Once we'd passed the coast of southern England, we flew above cloud so apparently solid that penguins or polar bears wouldn't have been out of place. As it thinned, there were glimpses of a twinkling ocean creaming below and, later, a finger of land edged with sandy beaches – Denmark, I supposed – then more sea, sometimes veiled by drifting cloud. Quite suddenly the sea was freckled with hundreds of tiny islands, just scattered like sugar strands on top of a vast blue cake, and mainland Sweden was only minutes away.

I walked out of customs to a smiling, unchanged Ann. We hadn't met face to face for nearly twenty years but it didn't seem to matter, and after the first hug and a very few tentative words, we relaxed. By the time Ann had driven the half hour to her home, we were chatting and laughing as we had in our teens. It was both easy and difficult to talk, as we had so much to catch up on. We were also both conscious that we wanted to talk about our mothers and the reason for my visit, but it didn't seem right to launch into anything serious so soon. Fortunately this inhibition didn't last long, and by the time we'd drunk cups of tea in Ann's comfortable kitchen no topic was off limits.

I met her three children, Petter (17), David (15) and Hanna (12), and marvelled at their excellent English. Bengt, Ann's husband, smiled dismissively at my attempts to learn Swedish, saying, "You would learn Swedish in three weeks – but Hazel, you're only here for two, so don't bother!" Nonetheless, my efforts at Swedish pronunciation caused constant hilarity, and Bengt was not the only one to tease me. "Say 'sjukhus', ('hospital') they would demand and I'd twist my tongue into a spiral in an effort to imitate them accurately as they laughed. Petter quickly rechristened me 'Roland Hassel', a cartoon detective on Swedish television – and I felt part of the family.

That evening Jaan, Ann's brother, came unexpectedly, and I looked in vain for the little boy whose embroidered braces I'd admired so long ago. Jaan, Ann and I talked easily and I was touched when Jaan said that he'd always known us. So that special bond was not just something Mum had influenced *me* to feel.

How do you sleep when so many new impressions, questions and emotions are rattling around in your brain? How do Scandinavians sleep anyway when it's light enough to weed the garden all night? I must have drifted off eventually but it was certainly a busy night in my head, and at about five I was woken by a strange sound, like a dragon's fiery breath. I leapt to the window and caught sight of a hot air balloon lifting high above the trees.

The sea was just a short walk away, not the sort of shore familiar to us around much of our coast, but more reminiscent of a Scottish loch. I was totally unprepared for what a watery place Stockholm is: islands, inlets, boats, tree-lined shores, but no tides to speak of and very little salt in the water. A car tour of Stockholm in the evening passed in a blur of bridges, rocky outcrops, buildings and more water. We ate ice cream high above the old dock with a splendid view of old and new Stockholm and I saw where the huge freshwater Lake Mälaren joins the faintly salty Baltic, and learned that all Swedes have the right to fish there.

It was a sparkling two weeks, as memorable to me as Mum's visit to Estonia was for her. I wandered around Stockholm both alone and with Ann, who'd made sure I could use the bus and the underground. She was working as an anaesthetist in one of the hospitals, but had generously taken some time off while I was there. The children and Bengt were horrified that I'd spent about five hours in the Historiska Museet, a museum of Viking antiquities. "What on earth did you find to do there?" asked Petter in amazement. My passion for all things Viking was delightfully fed by the local road names: Odinsvägen, Midgårdsvägen and Sveavägen. That amused them too.

On another of my solo trips to Stockholm, I browsed in the National Gallery, where I enjoyed a number of Impressionist paintings and made the acquaintance of Carl Larsson, a painter – some would argue 'only' an illustrator – whose pictures are a delightfully idealised representation of Swedish family life a hundred or so years ago. They really appealed to me then. A 'Decor through the ages' exhibition was less attractive, and

I giggled inwardly in front of a sculpture of a pair of black wellington boots – looking, admittedly, very rubbery and inhabited – treading on a heap of eggs which spewed yolk, white and shell down the pile. Now, in the twenty-first century this would appear fairly run-of-the-mill, but then it was distinctly unusual.

Ann took me to Hanna's school finishing ceremony, which was attended by many mothers and fathers who took time off for this occasion as a matter of course. I wondered how many English bosses would be sympathetic to their workers arriving late because of school assembly. The parents joined emotionally with the children in singing the summer hymn which is sung in every Swedish school on this day, and I was surprised to find myself quite moved by it. There was something very touching about their appreciation, without any sense of irony, of a tradition which had punctuated their own schooldays.

As an end-of-school treat for Hanna and David, we went into Stockholm for lunch at a very exclusive market hall café, then to a superb museum of sculptures by Carl Milles. They were mostly displayed in the gardens of his waterside house on lofty pedestals or in the middle of pools. Lovely fluid, airy shapes cavorted against a backdrop of busy Stockholm across an expanse of water.

There were other trips, largely without the children, through miles of green farmland and forest, past wooden houses coloured dark red by the copper-based paint which preserves the wood so well, past tall spikes of drying hay, fields of sleek brown horses, and on to Uppsala and Old Uppsala, where we picnicked on the ancient grave mounds of the kings. We stopped for my benefit at Mora Stenar, where kings were once elected, though there's little to see now except a few rune stones and flat, flat meadows, once the seabed.

In more rolling countryside we visited Linné's Hammarby, the farmhouse of Linnaeus, father of botanical classification. The house and buildings are furnished very simply, but what I remember most clearly was a glass-fronted cabinet full of Linnaeus's folders of pressed flowers. There was no barrier or notice to stop you opening the door and leafing through one of these. His wife must have been a very competent lady, as she was left to run the farm while her husband swanned off to foreign parts and, presumably, wedded himself to his specimens when at home. Perhaps Mrs Linné preferred it that way.

Another drive was through the suburbs of Stockholm, very green with the blocks of flats widely spaced, to Drottningholm Palace, where the present king and family live for most of the year. It's an imposing but very public building, right by the water thronged with boats, and all but a tiny formal area of the garden and park are open to the public. On then through lush meadows and across ferries to a series of islands on a Lake Mälaren, to a point where we could see Birka on Björkö, an important archaeological site for Viking scholars and the centre of one of the earliest Christian missions to Scandinavia. I couldn't believe how tiny and isolated the island was. It lay tantalisingly across a glassy expanse of water. We'd missed the only ferry. In compensation Bengt found me a twelfth-century church, another runic stone and an ancient burial ground, where we sat high on a long barrow and ate our lunch, gazing across what had once been a harbour to the water beyond and the islands.

There were boat trips too in the family boat, both into Stockholm and away through the islands. I was again amazed at the mass of inlets, with shorelines sometimes low and sometimes rocky but quite smoothly contoured with shallow cliffs. As there are few high winds and the sea isn't very salty, oak, beech, silver birch and fir trees thrive right down to the water's edge in a way that isn't possible in most of England. Holiday houses with verandahs and boat anchorages lined some islands, and many families cruised around the archipelago on summer weekends, landing wherever they liked. Apparently, in winter the sea is frozen and many people skate to work in the city, but on such a warm summer day it was hard to imagine. I'm not sure that this is true now with the weather changes brought on by global warming.

I tasted lingonberries and cloudberry ice cream. (Surely Cloudberry was the name of a gnome in B.B.'s story 'The Little Grey Men'.) They took me to a friend's herring tasting party, where we ate at a long table in the garden and food was interrupted by singing and schnapps drinking. I tasted reindeer, laxpudding, new potatoes with dill, filmjölk and caviar-like bright amber jewels. Ann rhapsodised over the sensation of bursting each little globule against your palate, while Bengt told me it was essential to puncture every one to avoid them hatching out. Somehow I couldn't stomach all mine after that, and passed them on to Bengt, which was probably what he intended.

And there was Meta.

Meta in 1989

To come face to face with Meta again, as an adult and not as a gauche student, was exactly what I wanted, but when the moment arrived, I felt a sense of panic. She was Mum's dear friend, not mine. Could I love her enough to compensate for Mum's absence? My questions might seem like an intrusion rather than a desire to celebrate their friendship. How would I explain to Meta what I was trying to do? Did she still feel the same warmth towards Mum or had she filed her memory away along with unimportant things?

I needn't have worried. Meta had her anxieties too, but they were far more practical than mine. She very much wanted to see me but was full of doubts about her rusty English, and it still amazed her that I should find her interesting. She had so little confidence. How like Mum.

Our first conversations were slow and emotional, but as Meta relaxed, her English returned more fully with each meeting. Petter and David were touchingly anxious that these meetings would be fruitful, and David provided me with a tape recorder so that I needn't take notes all the time.

Together we looked at photographs. I wanted to introduce Meta to my family and to show her some of the last pictures of my parents. With me too were copies of the snapshots, diary and map from Mum's visit to Estonia – and Meta's letters to Mum. She didn't want to see the letters. "I am a different person now," she said. But the other things interested her enormously. She identified people and places, laughed as photos triggered memories, and took home to show Henno the most evocative ones.

When we next met it was at their flat, a pleasant, light-filled place with a living room lined with books and African violets on every windowsill. Henno was able to greet me too, though sickness and long lack of use had deprived him of most of his English. They seemed keyed up and excited, and Meta explained how the pictures and the diary had made them talk about things they'd forgotten long ago. Henno had recognised one picture as the place where they'd spent their honeymoon. There were people too whom they'd forgotten completely and were glad to think of again. It seemed to have released good recollections for them. I was relieved to see them laugh together as the diary triggered other happy memories. I'd been so afraid it would make them sad. "We only really had one year," Henno said wistfully, meaning the year together in Estonia after they were married. Mum was part of that year too.

Before I left them that afternoon, Meta handed me a folder of letters. Amazingly, this was the other side of the correspondence that I possessed – Mum's post-war letters to Meta – and Nan's. I'd had no idea that Meta had kept them. We met at Ann's house after that. I think Meta liked to have a specific reason to leave the flat, as she was very tied by Henno's progressing Parkinson's disease, but I'm glad I was able to meet him and to see their home.

Memories seldom come in chronological order, and Meta's were like a series of ill-sorted pictures that I'd half-seen before. She drew my eye to details I hadn't noticed and coloured in other unknown areas. One of the first things she said to me was: "The staying in London with your mother was the happiest time in my life." I was shocked. Was this really true? Later I was able to press her further on this, but I didn't like to do that in our first conversation, so discussed it with Ann instead. She'd heard her mother say this before, and began to explain to me how the time in England was the one time that Meta wasn't dominated by Mrs Lender. It was also the only time in her life, apart perhaps from her early childhood, when she lived in a united family, where there was give and take – spiced with irritability, but with everyone valuing the others for what they were.

In later talks with Meta, I asked her more about her time in England and began to understand just how much of her life was overshadowed by her mother-in-law. Eventually I couldn't help but ask her why on earth she'd agreed to lodge with the Lenders all those years ago when she was a student. She didn't answer for such a long time that I felt I'd made a mistake in asking – then she heaved an enormous sigh and said, "Well, it was very difficult. Mrs Lender was such a strong figure and always wanted her own way. It was too difficult to resist – I had been under her domination so long. I didn't want to go." She said this with such vehemence that tears sprang to *my* eyes; she was talking about feelings from over fifty years ago and they were still so very strong.

On another day, my indignation on Meta's behalf was so roused by yet another story – perhaps the wedding bouquet or the interference and complaints when they lived in Stocksund – that I blurted out "Did you *ever* like her?" There was only a slight pause before she answered rather quietly but very firmly, "No." It was as though Meta had never before dared to voice this feeling even to herself, for she was quick to add that she could see Mrs Lender's good points. She appreciated what she'd achieved for girls' education in particular and understood why many of her former pupils admired her. And, of course, she was Henno's mother.

But I didn't ask her why she hadn't confided any of this to Mum. At the time, I found this new picture of her mother-in-law difficult to assimilate, as Mum had always told me that at least Meta had some relatives in Sweden. The implication of her reticence didn't strike me until much later, when I read Mum's side of the correspondence and realised how many important things *she* kept from Meta.

In each conversation with her my knowledge of Meta's life expanded. I learned of her childhood and school life; the awfulness of being sent away from her mother to Tallinn; the difficulty of accepting her parents' marriage breakdown and the even greater trauma of sharing a home with her step-mother, an alcoholic; of her training as a teacher and the wonderful time with Mum in England and then in Estonia; of the escalating terrors brought by the war; and of their escape to Sweden. I was struck by the clarity of her memories and the calm way she related them. It was obvious that she'd repeated events in her head many, many times, and obvious too that she'd altered her attitude to some things. She no longer felt bitter about her father, and regretted losing the opportunity to tell him so.

I knew of her father's death in Siberia and of her brother Erik's survival, but now she told me a little more about Erik. He had eventually returned to their farm in Estonia to find their mother still alive. She survived until 1962 but Meta never saw her again, although she was able to write. For a long time Erik tried to get permission to travel to Sweden for a holiday. The Russian authorities wanted to know why his sister was there, and he concocted a story maintaining that German propaganda was so convincing in 1944 that she hadn't dared wait for the 'liberation' of the Russian invasion; he embroidered it further by saying the Germans had even threatened to shoot her if she didn't go to Germany. Of course, this was all completely untrue; but this, coupled with the fact that Erik had been in the Russian army (after many months avoiding conscription by living Robin Hood-like in the woods), led to him eventually being granted a travel pass on his second application.

Meta thought he was very much as she'd remembered him, but he found Meta changed. He told Ann how he always remembered Meta being so full of life and energy, always planning new things and doing them. She seemed so quiet and inert by comparison. I thought of her words to Mum: *I myself have lost much of my energy and goodwill. [...] Life had often been only a waiting that days pass quicker.* To Meta, Erik said, "Of course you were just a little girl when last we met." As Meta told me this, she smiled: "I was actually twenty-nine." She could smile and laugh with me but I was very conscious that this core of melancholy had never really left her.

I began to wonder just how much Mai, Ann and Jaan were affected by their parents' feelings. Meta stressed so often in her letters to Mum their desire to return to Estonia and with what reluctance she sent the children to a Swedish kindergarten: *We don't wish to stay here for ever – we should like to go back to our native country.* And a year later, when many Estonian refugees were going to Canada and USA, she wrote: *We don't want to leave Sweden. We hope we must not leave it before we go home. But where is our home? We refugees are people to whom a foreign land would never be a home and we are people whose old home is changed to a strange one when we can go back.* Even when they'd been in Sweden for six years she wrote: *I am sorry to tell you that I haven't any feeling it is my home or will be in the future. It is just living day after day and waiting for something else.*

I decided to ask Ann about her feelings towards Estonia and their upbringing. She couldn't tell me how Mai felt because it was not the sort of thing she would discuss with her. (I have never met Mai, who is married to an Estonian–Swede, the son of another refugee family, and may well not share Ann's attitude.) But Ann could confidently speak for herself and Jaan, and said they continued to bear the weight of their childhood and carried into their adult life a sense of not belonging. They feel neither Estonian nor Swedish and find themselves, without intending to, referring to Swedes as 'they' – it just surfaces as an unconscious attitude. Despite this, they are both very happy in Sweden, and Ann is, of course, married to a Swede. It is rare for them to speak anything other than Swedish together, and Ann's children do not speak Estonian.

At the time of our conversations, both Ann and Jaan still harboured resentment that they had been brought up as Estonians in Sweden and were not encouraged to integrate but were, as they saw it, taught to be isolated and critical; they felt it has made their adult lives difficult, as they continued to be unsure of their cultural identity and it mattered to them. Yet in 1952 Meta wrote: *the children are happier, they don't remember their real home and they don't feel they are strangers here. I am glad for that.* I suppose as parents we're never really sure what our children are thinking and how much they are affected by our unspoken thoughts.

It was not just the sparseness of their lives but the constant fear of Russians that Ann remembers: *They* [Mai, Ann and Jaan] *ask me sometimes when* [if?] *there will be a new war – where shall we go? When* [if?] *the Russians are coming to Sweden – what will happen? I cannot answer because I dare not think of that.* Meta may again be confusing 'when' with the German 'wenn', which gives different emphasis to this, but even so, I hadn't thought of them as being frightened in Sweden, although I recall Meta's comment to Mum when they first moved to Borås: *Henno is delighted of that idea to go to live in West Sweden. [...] We do not know how long will Russia be as far as that and then it is better to have the open sea to take a voyage to some other free country.* My childhood was overshadowed by my mother's wartime experiences – by her guilt, her horror of physical violence and of being parted from people she

197

loved – but there was never *fear*. I was always secure.

Ann told me that, for her, the long visits to us were very important. She found with us a sort of haven and loved being part of a normal busy family, thoroughly entrenched in its own country, with none of the burdens and fears which refugee status brings. With us she felt a security and ease which was very influential in resolving and smoothing her childhood. She loved us all but without envy or resentment. It amazed and humbled me to hear this, as I hadn't understood before her emotional turmoil. We'd talked so freely since the first days of knowing each other, yet so much had obviously not been said. Perhaps it was only now that Ann recognised it herself. There is an intriguing ambivalence in Ann and Jaan's attitude to their past. Despite their resentments, I noticed while I was in Sweden that they both grasped at news from Estonia and hoped very much that I might find out more about their parents than they already knew; they still found that there were questions they didn't dare ask. They were excited by the lifting of so many restrictions in Estonia thanks to Gorbachev's philosophy of *glasnost* and *perestroika*.

Some months before I went to Sweden, Ann accompanied a colleague, an orthopaedic surgeon, to Riga in Latvia as his anaesthetist. This was where she was when I wrote asking her to approach Meta for me – the letter that was put aside and hidden for so long. She leapt at the chance to go to Latvia because it gave her the possibility of travelling back through Estonia. It was an emotional experience being on Estonian soil for the first time since she was a small child, and she couldn't really describe it. But in Tallinn she found herself less interested in the sights of the city than in scanning the faces around her and simply stopping Estonians in the street and asking to photograph them.

Jaan was there when Ann told me this, and I asked him if he wanted to go to Estonia. "I've been there already in 1976," he told me quietly, although he only had permission to visit Tallinn. At that time the people weren't prepared to talk very much, and they certainly wouldn't have relished being accosted by a stranger from Sweden with a camera. I was curious to know how he felt being in Estonia for the first time – for he'd been born in Germany. He shrugged and smiled, then put both his hands to his head for a long time as he searched for words to express it. Ann nodded in agreement as he said, "It was like coming at last to my childhood."

In my final private conversation with Meta we talked of Mum and all our families, of England, Sweden, Estonia, bringing all the previous talks to one warm and satisfying conclusion. Our closeness had healed something for me; and, remembering there were questions that Ann and Jaan still wanted to ask, I shared with her Jaan's response to being in Estonia for the first time, hoping it might open a door to more conversations between them. There were tears in her eyes as she repeated, "Like coming at last to my childhood."

My long-cherished fantasies about Estonia didn't totally evaporate in the face of my visit to Sweden. True, there were apparently no cloud-capped towers and no particularly romantic mountain scenery, but the gorgeous palaces existed, as Meta showed me in a modern book of Estonian architecture. I could now visualise the Estonian countryside, as Meta said it was very similar to their part of Sweden. An enormous map of Estonia which Ann gave me made the country seem real – and indisputably flat. I would still have preferred a Bavarian or Transylvanian landscape, but had to accept the truth and put away my fond imaginings.

Incredible events took place in the communist world shortly after I left Sweden. In November 1989 the Berlin Wall came down. Gorbachev resigned from the Communist Party. In Estonia, Tartu University had Lenin's bronze statue melted down to be recast in the form of the university's founder, King Gustavus Adolphus. Fifty-two years earlier, Mum had signed the visitors' book in the university library there. On September 4th 1991, the Soviet President, Boris Yeltsin, issued a decree recognising the independence of the Baltic States: Latvia and Lithuania – and Estonia. Four days later Leningrad was renamed St. Petersburg, as it had been when Meta was young.

In June 1990 a regular ferry service from Stockholm to Tallinn was established, and Ann took Meta back for a short visit. It was not an easy few days. *Mum does not feel comfortable going back to Estonia – she avoids it which none of us children do. But maybe the memories are too strong for her.*

Henno died on 26th August 1991. Ann wrote: *We are going to bury Dad's ashes in Tallinn. It is something symbolic in the act – but you know Dad never liked Sweden and somehow never lived here either.* His ashes were finally interred next to his father, Voldemar, in May 1992.

Shortly after my Sweden visit, Ann brought Hanna to stay with us for the autumn half-term holiday. When I was in Sweden Hanna was very keen to talk with me, and by the time of this visit her English promised soon to be as good as Ann's. Her letters were lovely. We made Christmas puddings and cake together, including a very small cake to take back to share with Bengt, Petter, David – and dear Meta.

Estonia

My writing began thirty-two years ago on an old Amstrad machine, and I then transferred to a more modern one which used Word Perfect as its word processing programme. Later still a new processor and modern demands required Word. All of this occasioned somewhat laborious exercises to transpose and unify files. Meanwhile life somehow took over, and it was more than ten years after my visit to Sweden, as retirement age approached, that I began to wonder whether Ann would consider another visit to Estonia – with me this time. I really wanted to see some of the places mentioned in Mum's diary. It suddenly seemed possible. She replied enthusiastically almost by return of post and told me that Meta was also thrilled that I wanted to see Estonia for myself. So, on June 10th 2001, armed with a copy of Mum's diary, I met Ann at Tallinn airport. She picked up a hire car and we went straight to our hotel, where we talked and talked until we could no longer stay awake. In the square below, a colourful fair flourished, and the midnight fireworks seemed especially laid on for us.

My first view of Tallinn the next morning did not disappoint. Meta had shown me pictures of the old town in 1989, but the reality was even more pleasing. There were the walls of the citadel with the narrow, tall towers at its four corners, the twisty, cobbled street areas and the mellow colours of stone and roof tiles, the weathercocks and finials everywhere, pastel-painted frontages and decorative wooden doors. Sadly, peeling plaster and tarpaulins covered some key buildings, drainpipes finished yards from the ground and crumbling walls spoke of the neglect of maintenance under communism. Perhaps by now, as I write in 2022 (yes, still more time has elapsed), much of the renovation is complete and all restored to how Mum would have seen it. The tall spires and the onion domes of the Lutheran and Russian Orthodox churches were recognisable from Mum's photos and seemingly unchanged, despite the Soviet ban on religious practice. What a culture shock it all must have been to her; she'd never even been abroad before, except for a day trip to France as a schoolgirl, and had seen few pictures of Estonia. No wonder it enchanted her. I loved, as she had, the names of the two cobbled roads up the hill to Toompea, the citadel – Pikk Jalg (Long Leg) and Lühike Jalg (Short Leg) – and the affectionately named squat tower which now houses a museum – Fat Margaret.

The *posh coffee house in Independence Square* where Mum had so enjoyed her first Estonian coffee, 'served always with a glass of water', was no longer there, but we had coffee in a restaurant high up a tower and out onto a wooden terrace under a pitched roof, where incredibly tame and greedy sparrows joined us. Below, near the imposing concert hall, was a huge, open square, and Ann took me to see a bricked-up cellar nearby. It was here that those rounded up for deportation to Siberia were incarcerated. Among them were Henno's brother, sister and sister-in-law, and Meta's father. Later, in Pärnu, we saw flags at half-mast, bearing black ribbons commemorating their deportation on June 14th sixty years before.

Tallinn

Of the Houses of Parliament, Town Hall and other buildings flanking the main square I retain memories of glowing stone, pleasing proportions and architecture similar to other countries in the Hanseatic League. In Kadriorg Park outside the city walls, the baroque palace built for Peter the Great's wife, Catherine, was most imposing and was destined to house a gallery of Estonian art once renovations were completed. More memorable still was the very modest house a short distance away, where Peter the Great apparently stayed on his frequent visits to Tallinn during the building of the palace. All these things Mum had seen too…but we saw no *'black swans on the lake'.*

We did, however, see the Dalai Lama. Hundreds of people stood in the main square offering flowers and waving 'Free Tibet' flags as he entered the Town Hall accompanied by smiling priests and grim-faced officials and police. When he emerged, his speech, in English, emphasised the need to acknowledge that people are people everywhere; a predictably peaceable view of humankind. I'm not sure what the impact of this would have been on Estonian listeners, many of whom nursed decidedly antagonistic feelings towards the Russians who still lived among them.

In a shop we found a book written about Elfriede Lender's school, which included a number of photos, and I was charmed to see a 15-year-old Meta in one. In another was the teacher of the infants, Meta's supervisor, who had made her life so difficult – an enormous and intimidating woman with a sour expression. I'm not at all surprised that Meta had trouble with her.

Even more interesting to me was a walk through some older suburbs to a rather beautiful area of large wooden houses in tree-lined roads. There were a few gaps that had obviously been caused by bomb damage, but the area was largely still intact. Ann finally located on a corner a large, timber-clad building, much like its neighbours. This was number 16 Köhleri, where the Lender family had lived, in an extensive rented apartment on the third floor. I had mixed emotions thinking of Meta living unhappily there under her headmistress's roof, writing so many letters to Mum. But, I mused, she did at least meet Henno.

The Lenders spent time too on their family farm – indeed was Voldemar there most of the time? – at Pirita, a short distance from Tallinn, situated on a wide river where Meta, Henno and Mum rowed. The family house had largely been destroyed by fire but had obviously been imposing; this was evident even from the charred ruin. Until I visited it, I hadn't appreciated that it had been not just a farmhouse but included workers' housing – some of which was still there and occupied – and a guest house. The estate was quite extensive and new, substantial houses were now being built on it. Quite where in the main house Mum had stayed Ann didn't know, but the walk to the sea would have been just the same, as was the ruin of St Bridget's monastery, which was unusually unisex – something Mum didn't comment on in her diary. Tiny areas of living quarters were still visible, together with remnants of the huge church; amazingly, the monastery included a hypocaust system to warm the living quarters. It was good to think that both monks and nuns were not destined to shiver in the depths of winter.

After lunch overlooking the river, we took the same short path as Meta and Mum to the sandy beach which curved all the way to Tallinn, the city superbly silhouetted against the skyline. We would have liked to see Mum's *wonderful crimson sunset* but it was too early, and Ann took me instead to the enormous song festival stadium not far away. Songs and folk dancing had formed a very important part of maintaining and preserving the Estonian cultural identity during the Soviet years, and they are still very much part of their cultural life. A wide, grassy amphitheatre capable of seating a massive audience led the eye way down to the covered, shell-like stage built to house an astonishing 30,000 singers at once. I should love to see and hear that one day.

The road from Tallinn to Pirita runs only a few yards from the sea, and behind it the land rises quite steeply through pleasantly wooded areas and suburbs to a cemetery covering a vast area with well spaced pine trees, all immaculately cared for. This was where Henno's ashes were interred next to his father, Voldemar Lender, first mayor of Tallinn. As I write I remember Ann's words: *We are going to bury Dad's ashes in Tallinn. It is something symbolic in the act.*

We left Tallinn the next day and drove south to look for Meta's mother's home, but made a detour to Haapsalu, a town situated on a narrow spit of land and where Henno's cousin lived. *Spent topping afternoon in Uncle William's yacht*, Mum's diary declares, but she writes nothing more about it. It was apparently a favourite holiday place for the Tsar, who would perhaps have been appalled by the ugly apartment blocks now dwarfing the wooden houses and park. What Ann wanted me to see was the train station where Mum must have alighted. It was incredibly ornate for such a small place, and the platform was immensely long and specially roofed in to shelter the Tsar and his entourage. So – nothing changes when it comes to welcoming royalty and distinguished personages. I just hope that the townsfolk weren't impoverished as a result.

Ann and Hazel in Tallinn

Back on our original road south, we stopped to buy a drink in Kullamaa, where groups of men sat under lilac trees doing nothing at all but watching us curiously as we looked at a newish monument to the dead from 1941, including Meta's father, Kustas Tonkman. His farm had been nearby. Seeing his name there somehow made him seem real – I was going to say 'come alive' – and not just a name from Meta's story. It was from here that she went on horseback to catch the train in Risti (mentioned in the diary) to go to school in Tallinn.

The many wooden houses were overlooked by a tall-spired white church, large and dramatic for such a small town. Hideous blockwork buildings from the communist era contrasted starkly and were visible everywhere in the otherwise empty countryside, like rotting teeth. Apparently one effect at the end of communist domination was the abandonment of all their workshops and agricultural buildings – even those that were still useful. Ann read a possibly apocryphal tale of a six-storey building created by the communist regime in the middle of nowhere to house pigs. After a relatively short time it was abandoned since nobody had considered how to remove the dung.

On then to Üdrumaa, a mile or two further south, and the search for Meta's mother's old home at Vaiknal, too small to be marked on my map. Ann thought she'd found it just by the road; a half-wrecked, sad and abandoned wooden building with boarded-up windows; grass, saplings and bushes were growing up around it. Unsure, she tried to phone Meta but couldn't get through, so tried Jaan instead, who confirmed that this was the place. I was totally surprised by how overgrown it was – although it was, of course, sixty years since Mum had been there. It was also very basic, and I wondered what her reaction had been to its outside toilet and other 'rustic' inconveniences. No doubt it appealed to her sense of romance and adventure. Meta later explained to Ann that there had originally been another building opposite this one where Erik had his store, and this ruin was the main house, which was built for Meta's mother following the divorce and was where Mum had slept while Henno and Meta were in the hayloft of yet another building. Mum joined them there for a photo of the three of them smiling down.

I now realise with a slight shock that it was from here that Meta fled to Pärnu in the horse-drawn cart with Ann and Mai and so few belongings; it hadn't occurred to me when we were there. Their journey was agonisingly slow, because the horse could not be over-tired and it was seventy miles or more, a long way for a horse. But for Ann and me in the comfort of a car, that same route was easy, through mostly empty, flat countryside with extensive forests of birch and oak intermixed with pine, totally uncared for and choked with underbrush. In some fields a cow or two grazed, and a small, stripped area for vegetables or a thin crop of wheat spoke of underuse and agricultural decay everywhere. Ann had told me repeatedly what an empty country Estonia is, and I began to appreciate just what she meant; we had the road almost entirely to ourselves and saw no one in the fields. I also now understood how men, including Meta's brother, Erik, had been able to hide from the invading forces and from conscription in these woods, which cover so much of the country.

Pärnu looked fairly prosperous with its little port and marina and its pleasing park. It had been a favourite spa town for Russians for a long time and is still a spa, with various large, newly built hotels offering mud bath facilities and other curative or beauty treatments. In the maze of broad streets of the town were many wooden houses – mostly quite large, some well maintained and others in need of a facelift. It was here that Mum mistook their woman carriage driver for a man. Did she see the large, ornately painted arch called the Tallinn Gate, which was part of the original town and fortification and the gateway into Pärnu from the sea? Certainly the beautiful white sands were as she had enjoyed them, though it was sadly not the weather to relish a *lazy morning* there as they had done, or *a walk along moonlit sands.*

Beyond Pärnu was more empty countryside, with flower-filled verges and many small lakes fringed with rushes and, in one case, a wide margin of water lilies just coming into buttercup-yellow flower. An enormous, rich red-brown field was being worked by machines, evidently a peat field, peat being in places used for fuel. Ann had never seen this before. A delightful first for me was the sight of storks grazing in a field, with an untidy nest on top of a telegraph pole.

In Viljandi, Mum's lakeside town, we went into an astonishingly undeveloped shop or series of shops housed in prison cell-like rooms in a blank-faced warehouse building right on the street. This was apparently what most shops were like here in the past – either this or, as in this country, in the front room of a house. In some places noble attempts had been made to enlarge the windows and to display goods, but marketing seemed as yet a rather alien concept in smaller towns – a stark contrast to the modernity of Tallinn and Tartu.

I loved the story attached to a new-looking war memorial in a wide-open area in front of a shop in Rõngu. It commemorated the first War of Independence, 1918–21. In the winter of 1944, when snow had set in, the Russians had removed it from its plinth and laid it face down on the ground, but in the morning it had disappeared. There were stories circulating of a man pulling it away on a sledge drawn by a white horse. However, no-one in the neighbourhood had a white horse. Many years passed, then in 1988, as the Russian domination was beginning to relax, an old woman claimed to know where the stone was. It was her husband who had spirited it away, having covered his horse with whitewash to make it less visible in the snow. He took the stone home, washed off the horse, dug a large hole and put the stone in, subsequently building a sauna on top. How Mum too would have loved this story.

Our next destination was Tartu, but Ann made a detour to Otepää, where a church dominated a hilly area with pleasing fields and trees around. On the outside wall of the church was a plaque, in black relief on a white background, depicting three bearded young men saluting a flag. It was in commemoration of a group of students from Tartu University, thirty kilometres away, who had travelled to Otepää for an outing in 1884 and took with them the flag of their society and raised it there. This is thought by some to be the beginning of the movement to make Estonia a country and culture in its own right. It represented a nudge towards independence, and the flag – a horizontal stripe in blue, black and white – has been adopted as the country's own.

The city of Tartu is full of neoclassical buildings, and the main square was stunning in the sunshine. Here was more of my imagined fairy story vision, as the city rose away from the river Emajõgi: an expansive, cobbled area with tall, pastel-painted buildings to right and left and the imposing Town Hall ahead, with glimpses of a green park behind it – and in front a delightful fountain, centred around a statue of an embracing couple under an umbrella which dropped water from its ribs. The gaiety of their embrace had to raise a smile, and real children played around its rim.

I had been intrigued to read that Mum had signed the visitors' book in the university library – as had Goethe, she noted – and Ann was willing to see if we could track this down and perhaps add our signatures. The receptionists working in the university buildings were touchingly obliging in helping us with our search and sent us from one department to another, which involved considerable form-signing and one day ticket-issuing. In, around and through buildings old and new we walked – up narrow stairs, through creaking doors and in and out of spacious atriums and hushed corridors but, sadly, all to no avail…all negotiated with such patience and encouragement by officials who became increasingly apologetic as we were sent from one to another. Ann too was indefatigable in her explanations and tenacity – which I, of course, couldn't follow, since it was all in Estonian.

Defeated, we retired to a student café for lunch, and found on consulting Mum's diary that it was the same one that Mum and Meta had visited. To my surprise I felt suddenly emotional, and in analysing this I realised that I was saddened to feel that I had never shared a time when Mum was completely happy, but had only known her when encumbered with the guilt and the lack of confidence which overshadowed so much of her life. In discussing this with Ann, we both acknowledged that this holiday with Mum and Henno was part of the short space in Meta's life when she too felt happy and totally relaxed.

To deflect us from this was the sight of uniformed choirs beginning to assemble for the song and music festival which was to take place the next day. From our seat we spotted a fairly young group of fifty or so people being put through energetic breathing exercises by their conductor, who was facing us. I said there was surely going to be a little bad behaviour from the young ones in the back row, and sure enough we were treated to an amusing pantomime by a couple of boys mimicking the conductor's wide gestures, securely out of his sight.

Away from the university buildings and the imposing main square were interesting side roads, some with very big and ornate wooden houses and others, not even tarmacked, with smaller homes which looked much as they had a hundred years before. We were amused at several mistranslations in places, including the "backside of a hill" and "the Russians went backwards over the bridge", which rather detracted from the seriousness of a well-known defeat and retreat. Several times our search for the elusive visitors' book took us past a large ruin emblazoned with a notice saying "Be cautious! The building is liable to fall down!" Fortunately, it remained intact each time we passed.

From then on the holiday was ours alone, as we were not going to Finland for the day as Mum had, nor were we visiting Narva on the north-eastern border of Estonia with Russia. There was huge satisfaction in having found the landmarks from the diary but now Ann could show me other things, and there was a sense of liberation and relaxation of tension in this. Not bound by public transport, we were able to set off north from Tartu along a road which eventually ran alongside Lake Peipsi, which lies on the border between Russia and Estonia – the fifth-largest lake in Europe. On that day it lay glassily still, just occasionally ruffled by a slight wind causing tiny wavelets. Small wooden houses with little vegetable patches and beautifully stacked woodpiles were scattered along the road and in the unmade tracks off to the side. At intervals an old man or woman sat behind a table or simply on the ground, perhaps accompanied by a dog, selling fish or courgettes. I wondered how many sales they would get, as the road was so empty of traffic.

After stopping briefly in the lakeside towns of Kallaste – a new place name for me – we left the lake and turned north to the northern sea coast of Estonia, skirting the fringe of a flat, unattractive industrial area with slag heaps from phosphate mines, and then detoured to Kuremäe and the Russian Orthodox convent of Pühtitsa. It was founded in 1891 but the area was considered a holy site from much earlier times, following a vision of the Virgin Mary and the discovery of an icon beneath an oak tree and a spring with life-giving properties. When we were there 160 nuns lived and worked in the small, green-roofed houses and tended the beautiful gardens awash with peonies, lilacs and deutzia. Amazingly, this convent escaped obliteration under communism, although at times the larger buildings were used as a hospital and a children's home. It has subsequently sent sisters throughout Russia to establish religious houses. We saw some of them, black-clad, going quietly about their lives. One was stacking logs on an astonishing woodpile next to two or three completed ones which dwarfed her, towering perhaps thirty feet high, wonderfully crafted in a cylindrical shape twenty feet or more in diameter and topped with a neat cone of logs. They were amazing feats of craftsmanship and it seemed a shame that they would have to be dismantled when the fuel was needed.

Peace more to my taste was the night spent at the newly built wooden home of friends of Ann's brother-in-law, Mart, on the fringe of the Lahemaa National Park in a quiet glade among forest trees and not far from the sea, which on that day was placidly still and blue, edged by a sandy margin with rocks dotting the shallows. The park covers a large part of the north of the country and is an area of woods and meadows not very unlike much of the rest of Estonia. In a leaflet we read of various forest trails and the haunts of beaver, elk, wild boar and – shades of my fairy story imaginings – bears. On our woodland walk we saw swathes of large white anemones and massive scotch pines and heard jubilant birdsong – but no bears, despite Ann calling out to summon them.

By this time we had just about circumnavigated the whole country, and I was impressed by Ann's knowledge of Estonia and her obvious pleasure in showing it to me. She seldom seemed to consult a map but pored over it with me on the last day, highlighting the route we had taken. It is, as she had kept reminding me, a small, empty country with few significant areas of high ground and huge swathes of woodland. But even in the short time we were there, I had begun to appreciate the scenery, so very different from my home on Dartmoor.

Back in Tallinn at the end of our trip, my brain fizzed with kaleidoscopic images of buildings, restored manor houses, small wooden thatched houses, quiet seashores, erratic boulders, storks, bears and meals of delicious dried fish, wild boar, pirogi and black bread. I recalled people with bags of small, round doughnuts in Tartu, bright red dyed hair in Tallinn, flower sellers everywhere and endless cups of coffee – not necessarily served with a glass of water. By now I understood why Mum's diary had petered out, as there was so much to absorb. Fortunately I had kept a much more comprehensive journal, which I wrote in each night.

We had a last walk round a now familiar Tallinn; I do hope it hasn't been spoiled by the influx of tourists since we were there. To go our separate ways was immensely difficult and our hugs were tearful as we said goodbye. We had talked so much and shared so many thoughts, both about ourselves and our mothers, and renewed the closeness we had always had. There was, though, a sense of completeness in having retraced that momentous visit which Mum had made in 1939 and to have given Meta the satisfaction of knowing that I too had appreciated her Estonia and now had memories of my own. For me their joint story was fleshed out and made real. Mum would have liked that.

Coda

Meta continued to live in Stockholm until her death in September 2012. Unfortunately her debilitating headaches still occurred and were inevitably depressing. Ann, Mai and Jaan visited her with unfailing regularity, but I never managed to see her again. My only written contact with her was with birthday and Christmas cards or messages via Ann.

Very sadly, Mai and Ann's lovely brother, Jaan, died too in 2014 – far too young and, like Meta, much missed.

Phyllis – Mum – died twenty-five years earlier than Meta, in September 1987. She had never really recovered from Dad's death. The final parting from him was something she had always dreaded, and what little confidence she had gained over the years evaporated when he died. She enjoyed times with all three of our families but would never stay for many days, however tempting it felt, as she knew how hard it was to return to a house without George.

A fall in her house caused damage to the hip replaced in 1969, and she suffered many weeks in hospital on traction, but never regained full mobility. Her last few weeks were spent in a nursing home, in pain, and gradually retreating as small strokes affected her comprehension. Rosa was too far away to be there, but Pete and I sat on either side of her for part of her last few days and nights, talking quietly. Mum wasn't really there – it wasn't her any more propped up on that bed – only the long, tapering fingers were unmistakably hers. We left, finally, in the early hours of her last night, too tired to stay longer. The nurses suggested that by leaving we enabled her to let go of life at last. But I felt guilty that we hadn't stayed longer.

However, the days that followed were surprisingly happy ones as we three children drew close together. We were a little embarrassed to find the funeral a pleasing occasion. It was good to see so many friends and wider family, and together we shared memories and experiences. We talked and laughed but few tears were shed, as her death was really a release. Mum would have been surprised to realise just how many people loved her.

The clearing of the house inevitably took a long time, as both Mum and Dad had been hoarders of everything, from jam jars to payslips. We sifted and sorted hundreds of books and papers, and it was one morning when I was there on my own that I came across the letters from Meta, the catalyst for this book. I wept a little as I read them – tears for Meta and, at last, for Mum.

My interest in all things Estonian was re-ignited and I spent many hours trying to track down books and information, much of which was available only at the British Library. How much easier it is now with the Internet and Wikipedia. Our move to Dartmoor in 1988 caused me to put all this to one side, but I did begin to write even then, and to plan the shape of this book, hoping one day to have time to complete it. Little did I dream that it would take so long.

Sadly, Ann and I have not often met since our trip to Estonia, as our respective lives have engulfed us. She and Bengt came to stay one year, and in 1983 Ann came again on her own. After each meeting we wrote fairly frequently to begin with; then, as technology came within our grasp, emails took over, but we are not exactly regular correspondents. Unlike Mum and Meta, we are not leaving a vast paper trail. I think we both now understand why our mothers' letters became increasingly sparse as time went on. Life has a way of taking over as children grow and grandchildren appear. Illnesses occurred in both of our families, and holidays were taken, celebrations enjoyed – much of which we relayed to each other. We both know, however, that the depth of our friendship transcends distance, and we would be able to talk and talk very easily again when face to face. Perhaps we can one day put that to the test.

Now, most days I think of Ann and, indeed, I usually check in our newspaper for the weather forecast in Stockholm. It gives me pleasure to imagine her in sunshine or rain…all under the same sky that embraces me.

Acknowledgements

I am very grateful to Elisabeth Rowe, whose invitation to join the 'Inkspots' and whose reading of the first draft of this book gave me the impetus and courage to resume writing after a lapse of many years. Thanks also to fellow Inkspotters, Karen Hayes and Trish Dugmore, for introducing me to SilverWood.